NARCISSISM

2 books in 1:

NARCISSISTIC ABUSE

&

EMOTIONAL INTELLIGENCE

How to deal with a narcissistic partner or emotionally immature parents

(disarm the narcissist and heal yourself)

© Copyright 2019 - All rights reserved.

The content contained within this book may not be reproduced, duplicated or transmitted without direct written permission from the author or the publisher.

Under no circumstances will any blame or legal responsibility be held against the publisher, or author, for any damages, reparation, or monetary loss due to the information contained within this book. Either directly or indirectly.

Legal Notice:

This book is copyright protected. This book is only for personal use. You cannot amend, distribute, sell, use, quote or paraphrase any part, or the content within this book, without the consent of the author or publisher.

Disclaimer Notice:

Please note the information contained within this document is for educational and entertainment purposes only. All effort has been executed to present accurate, up to date, and reliable, complete information. No warranties of any kind are declared or implied. Readers acknowledge that the author is not engaging in the rendering of legal, financial, medical or professional advice. The content within this book has been derived from various sources. Please consult a licensed professional before attempting any techniques outlined in this book.

By reading this document, the reader agrees that under no circumstances is the author responsible for any losses, direct or indirect, which are incurred as a result of the use of information contained within this document, including, but not limited to, — errors, omissions, or inaccuracies.

Table of contents

- BOOK 1 8
- NARCISSISTIC ABUSE 8
- *Part I: Narcissistic Personality Disorder* 15
- *Chapter 1: Understanding Narcissists and Narcissistic Personalities* 15
  - Causes and diagnosis 17
  - Characteristics of narcissistic personalities 20
- *Chapter 2: Types of Narcissists* 33
  - Classic narcissists 33
  - Vulnerable narcissists 34
  - Malignant narcissists 35
  - Overt and covert narcissists 36
  - Somatic and cerebral narcissists 37
  - Inverted narcissists 38
- *Chapter 3: Narcissistic Manipulation Techniques* 40
- *Part II: Narcissism In Relationships* 58
- *Chapter 4: How to Handle a Narcissistic Partner* .. 58
  - Four-point framework for dealing with a narcissist .. 59
  - Tips for dealing with a narcissist 68
- *Chapter 5: Effects of Narcissism in Relationships* 73
  - Why am I attracting narcissists? 75
  - Why empaths attract narcissists 80

Part III: Surviving Narcissistic Abuse 86

Chapter 6: Psychological Violence on Victims of Narcissistic Abuse 86

Children and Families 89
Relationships 94
Narcissism among friends 102
Workplace narcissism 104

Part IV: Self-Healing 107

Chapter 7: Healing from Narcissistic Abuse 107

Meditation 107
Group therapy 109
Cognitive behavioral therapy 111
Cognitive processing therapy 112
Yoga 114
Art therapy 116
EMDR 117
Self-hypnosis 118
Aromatherapy 120

Chapter 8: Developing Emotional Intelligence After Narcissistic Abuse 123

Fundamentals of recovery from narcissistic abuse . 128
Resetting boundaries after surviving a narcissist ... 132

Conclusion 138

BOOK 2 143
EMOTIONAL INTELLIGENCE 143
Introduction *144*
Chapter 1: What Is Emotional Intelligence and How it Affects Your Relationships *148*
Elements of Emotional Intelligence **150**
Self-Awareness 150
Self-Regulation 151
Social Skills 152
Empathy 153

Chapter 2: Why Being in Tune with Your Emotions Can Significantly Improve Your Life in All Areas 156
Enhances Physical Health 157
Improves Mental Health 158
Leads to Better Relationships 158
Conflict Resolution 159
Increased Success 160
Improved Leadership Skills 161

Chapter 3: How You Can Boost Your EQ *162*
Reduce Negative Emotions 163
Stay Cool 164
Adopt an Assertive Way of Communication 165
Active Listening 165
Label Your Emotions 166
Take Critique Positively 166
Show Empathy 167
Be Accountable for Your Emotions 167
Take Note of Other People's Feelings 168
Determine Whether Your Feelings are Friendly 169
Track Your Progress 170

Chapter 4: Learn to Deal with Your Feelings *171*
Suppressing Your Feelings 171
Timeouts 173

Stop and Think...174
See the Bigger Picture..174
Understand Your Emotions..175
Pardon Your Emotional Triggers 176
Find Healthy Outlets..176

Chapter 5: How to Control Negative Emotions 178
Eliminate Negative Thoughts...179
Overcome Stress and Anxiety 181
Overcome Social Anxiety and Shyness... 183

Chapter 6: Tips and Strategies to Improve/Rescue Relationships in Both Your Work and Personal Life 188
Acknowledge and Celebrate Differences 189
Listen Effectively 190
Give People Time..191
Improve Your Communication Skills 192
Manage Mobile Technology 193
Feedback.. 194

Chapter 7: Communicate More Effectively 195
Active Listening...195
Non-Verbal Cues... 196
Manage Your Stress..197
Assert Yourself 197
Keep it Simple.. 198

Chapter 8: Develop Social Awareness and Build Strong and Meaningful Relationships...................200
Develop Empathy 201
Evaluate Social Cues 201
Connect with Your Community...202

Chapter 9: Improve Your Social Skills 203
Improve on Verbal Communication 203
Tweak Your Non-Verbal Communication.......................................204
Connect with the Real World 205
Practice Makes Perfect...205

Chapter 10: Improve and Enhance Empathy: Connect Naturally With Others 207
  What is Empathy? 207
  Common Traits of an Empathic Person 208
  Improving Your Empathy 209
  How Highly Sensitive People Manage Their Emotions 211
  Understanding the Potential of Being Empathic, Controlling Overwhelming Feelings 214

Final Thoughts 220

Bibliography 223

BOOK 1
NARCISSISTIC ABUSE

Disarm the narcissist and take back your life after covert emotional abuse - Survive toxic relationships, a narcissistic mother, borderline personality types

(narcissism recovery)

Introduction

When we mention "narcissism" we usually think about people who are obsessed with appearances. This basic concept takes away meaning from something deeper, a mental disorder. Narcissistic personality, like many other mental disorders, is a confusing subject. Many of the patients who suffer might not be aware of what they are doing, while some others are fully aware of what they want and ready to take advantage from their manipulative abilities.

Victims of narcissistic abuse usually bear scars deeper and more hurtful than any physical scars you might come across. Emotional scars last a lifetime for some people. They might not have harmed you physically, but the impact on your life will stay with you forever. As you read this book, you will learn a lot about narcissism, the narcissist, and the victim. These three are important concepts that will form your understanding of the disorder, and help you figure out how to handle different situations involving any of them.

This book is written in four parts, each focusing on a unique aspect of dealing with narcissism. In the first part, we talk about narcissistic personality disorder. There is a lot that people don't know about narcissistic personality disorder, and narcissism. How do you tell whether someone is a narcissist or if they are simply too confident and assured about themselves?

Narcissists have some unique characteristics that define their personality. When you understand these traits, it is easier for you to recognize the difference between a narcissist and someone who oozes insane confidence. You must be careful, however, because some narcissists are so good at concealing their true selves, and can swoop in at your time of need and consume your life.

Beyond narcissistic traits, it is also a good idea to dig deep into some of the manipulative ways narcissists take over your life. Your life is all you have. If someone were to take it away, what else do you have? Life is such a precious thing, you must guard yours as jealously as you can. There is a lot of learning involved in understanding narcissistic personality disorder. One thing that you should keep at the back of your mind is that to a narcissist, no one and nothing else matters. Everything must be about them.

In the second part of this book, we take our discussion to an environment that has harbored narcissistic abuse since the beginning of time: relationships. There are different kinds of relationships, each of which perpetuates narcissism in its own way. Relationships are founded on trust. Whether professional or otherwise, you need to believe that your partner in the relationship reciprocates the trust you place in them, and in the relationship.

To show you just how serious narcissism is, and the damning effect it can have on your life, we look at the effect that narcissism has on children. Growing up in a family of narcissists can have significant effects on children. The trauma they live through defines the rest of their life. Everything about their life changes. This also affects their future relationships and their perception of a genuine relationship.

Romantic relationships are another venue where narcissism has crippled lives. Romance is full of turbulence. Narcissistic romance is confusing, especially when it happens between a narcissist and an empath. From the moment they meet each other, it feels like they are two people who were meant for each other. Their needs almost align and they become the perfect fit in front of their friends and family members. Unfortunately, that wounded animal is just that, an animal. What did they teach you about picking up stray animals, huh? – *they bite!*

Relationships today are largely superficial. It is not easy to tell a genuine relationship from a fake one. Everyone seems to be working towards something different, so you may wonder whether people ever have common goals anymore. However, relationships are beautiful. Healthy relationships are.

In the third part of this book, we introduce narcissistic abuse. This section is essentially about the victim. Narcissistic abuse is one of the worst forms of psychological torture. Many victims who have lived through this have harbored scars that last a lifetime. When they tell their stories, you can feel the pain in their voices. Even for people who have rebuilt their lives and are happy, you can still feel the fear in their voices when they relive their ordeals. Narcissistic abuse is a beast.

The kind of abuse victims live through leaves behind emotional and psychological scars. Imagine loving someone with everything you have, only for them to leave you nothing but a shell of yourself. You can barely recognize yourself by the time you get the courage to walk out of such a relationship.

Self-doubt, self-mutilation, self-sabotage, lack of self-esteem, losing confidence, anxiety, depression, and suicidal thoughts are not pretty. We might discuss them lightly on social media these days, but the reality is anything but pretty. It takes a lot of pain and hurt to turn someone who was once a happy and jovial soul into a depressed and suicidal person. Someone has to break you to a point where there is nothing more to break, for you to get to that point. It takes an animal, bereft of soul, to damage another person like that.

In the last part, we embrace healing. The journey through narcissistic abuse is not an easy one. Healing from the trauma is not easy either, but it is doable. Many people have been there, survived and lived to tell their story. At times it feels as if you are drowning. Your world is filled with unending darkness and you can't figure out the difference between day and night. All this shall pass.

There are many alternatives you can consider for recovery against narcissistic abuse. You have to trust in the process, and trust in your ability to see things through to the end. Remember how amazing your life was before this ordeal. Remind yourself of the joy, the goodness of your heart, happiness and sunshine that was your life back then. It might seem like it all went away, but it didn't. You just need to rediscover yourself.

Your way back after narcissistic abuse involves rediscovering your self-esteem, learning to set clear boundaries and more importantly, developing self-control. It is by reconnecting with your authentic self that you can remember what life was like before it was whisked away from you. You learn how to get your life back on track and steer it in into a future of success.

While writing this book, the resounding message in my mind was resilience. Life is unfair. Bad things seem to befall some of the nicest people on the planet. A narcissist is not someone you can change, but you can understand them. You can understand yourself and know when you need to walk away. You have to be resilient to realize your dreams. If you are knocked down, you won't stay down forever. In life, you love, you lose, you learn. Some of the challenges you experience in life set you on the path to real healing and greater things. However, you don't always have to learn the hard way.

There is so much more to live for, so much to achieve, and many dreams to fulfill. Get a hold of your life. Be, and stay in control.

Part I: Narcissistic Personality Disorder

Chapter 1: Understanding Narcissists and Narcissistic Personalities

Everyone loves attention, some more than others. Admiration, feeling important, feeling special. Wouldn't it be amazing if someone made you the center of his universe? All these are emotions and sentiments that people go through from time to time. The desire to feel special is normal. Everyone experiences it at some point. You might even go out of your way and do things for yourself that make you feel amazing.

What happens when things get out of hand? The desire to feel special turns into manipulation, cockiness and wanton desire to have everything going your way? At this point, it is no longer about being the center of attention, it might be something else, a mental disorder. You might be suffering from narcissistic personality disorder (NPD).

NPD is a serious condition. People don't talk about it a lot because it only affects roughly 1% of the global population (Wright & Furnham, 2015). Individuals who suffer from NPD have an inflated desire to enjoy all the feel-good feelings described above, usually at the expense of others. The lack of empathy sets in, and everything about the individual becomes exaggerated. Some of the things that mean the world to such individuals include vanity, prestige, power, and fame.

Like most mental conditions, NPD can be confusing because the symptoms might also be observed in people who are genuinely self-confident, or have a high self-esteem. Perhaps one of the differences between such individuals and those who suffer from NPD is that even with the confidence and esteem sky high, they somehow remain humble. On the other hand, people with NPD are boastful, selfish and will do everything in their power to get attention. Their needs must always come first.

On the surface, it is easy to assume that someone who portrays the definitive symptoms of NPD is overconfident and strongly believes in their abilities (Wright & Furnham, 2015). However, this is no more than a smokescreen for deeply rooted insecurity. Their insecurities are noticeable especially when they are provoked, or when they are in a situation that looks like things will not go their way. This is when their manipulative skills come into play in an attempt to turn things in their favor.

Generally, if you are living with NPD, it will affect your life negatively. A wave of unhappiness fills you especially when you need people to recognize your effort, but they don't (Schroeter & Thomson, 2018). You can throw tantrums to get attention over things that most people would find mundane. The overly inflated sense of self-importance creates a persona that most people cannot tolerate. Before you know it, everything around you suffers. From your work to relationships, both personal and professional, people seem to avoid interacting with you.

It is not easy for people living with NPD because the disorder masks their ability to see the role they play in the circumstances that push people away from them. The damaging effects of NPD do not just affect the people you interact with, but it affects you too. When people cannot stand you, and always find a reason to move away from you, you feel unfulfilled, empty inside, and in some cases, worthless.

Causes and diagnosis

While experts believe that NPD might be a result of environmental and genetic factors at play, there is still no definitive cause. Genetics and the environment within which persons living with NPD operates offers a plethora of possible causes, making it impossible to point at the exact cause.

The symptoms of NPD that persist into adulthood start in the developmental stages of life, and by the time the individual matures, they fully embrace the traits. Conflict in interpersonal development might also be responsible for these traits, given that the individual struggles to see sense in some activities, sentiments, reactions, and responses towards them in life (Linden, 2010). The following are some of the destructive conflicts that might happen in life, resulting in NPD:

- A child accustomed to excessive praise about their abilities or looks.

- Lack of a realistic feedback mechanism to counter excessive admiration.

- Overindulgence by family and peers, making the individual feel too important.

- Unpredictable, unreliable and inconsistent parental or guardian care.

- Surviving childhood abuse.

- Living between extremes of intense praise and criticism for good and bad deeds.

- Learning how to manipulate people by mimicking peers and parents.

- Children born with highly sensitive temperament.

Experts believe that people living with NPD do not have the same amount of gray matter in their left anterior insula as normal people do. The left anterior insula is the part of the brain responsible for regulating compassion, emotions, empathy and cognitive faculties (Miller & Maples, 2012). With this deficiency, it is understandable that NPD patients will struggle to show or recognize these emotions even when it is the only possible emotion.

In prevalence rates, more men suffer from NPD than women. Around 70% of people diagnosed with NPD are men. NPD also affects younger people more than older people. People who suffer from NPD do not usually feel they have a problem. For this reason, while therapy is recommended, it is very difficult for them to seek help. It is important, however, to understand the difference between NPD and narcissistic personality type.

NPD is about extremes. Pushing the definitive traits a notch higher. Excessively looking to other people to praise you. Feeling unique, superior, keeping superficial relationships and showing low or no empathy at all. NPD is narcissism in its extreme form. It causes functional impairment, distress, and the effects last for a very long time.

Characteristics of narcissistic personalities

Are you in a relationship, personal or otherwise, with someone who feels they are better than everyone else, and demand attention and admiration all the time? Do you feel the individual is constantly condescending, insulting others if things are not done their way, but at the slightest hint of criticism or disagreement, they throw a fit? Chances are high that you might be dealing with a narcissist.

There are some unique characteristics that can help you identify people suffering from NPD. Most of the time, these individuals engage in a twisted kind of power play just to get their way. As their victim, you should learn how to identify these personalities from afar, and create healthy boundaries so that you can coexist without conflict.

Remember that people who have NPD are more likely to resist change (Jin-Won Yang & Seok-Man Kwon, 2016). They are okay with their behavior, and if anything, they feel you who is asking them to be accommodative, might have a problem. While you might feel it is okay to go along with the demands of a narcissist so that you can avoid their rage, coldness and tantrums, it is an unhealthy way to cope. In fact, you only make things worse by doing that because they realize they wield power over you.

The following are some of the symptoms that might alert you to the presence of a narcissist in your immediate environment:

- Self-importance

Narcissists are not just arrogant and vain, they have an unreal image of themselves. They feel superior to everyone and everything else. They believe they are special, and can only be understood by other special people, who are also the only people worthy enough to interact with them.

Narcissists love association with high-status things, places and people. They have no time for ordinary life. Since they believe they are better than everyone else, they feel it is only fitting that they get the royal treatment too, even if they have not done much to warrant it.

When discussing their personal achievements, narcissists will inflate their accomplishments to satisfy their ego (Bardi, 2015). Their description includes how people are lucky to have them in their lives, their contributions to people's lives and how great they are.

- Delusions of grandeur

Reality will never match the grandiose perception narcissists have of themselves. Bearing this in mind, they thrive on fantasy. Their world is full of self-deception, magic, distortion and illusions. Everything about their lives is a fantasy with one constant concept – their power, brilliance, unlimited success, and attractiveness. They have it all.

The importance of such fantasies is that they protect the narcissist from facing their reality, which is an empty life filled with shame and guilt. Anything factual that contradicts their idea of who they are must either be rationalized out of existence or ignored altogether. The same contempt is applied to things or people who threaten to burst their bubble of fantasy. This explains why people who interact with narcissists are always walking on eggshells.

- Entitlement and superiority

Narcissists have a predefined order of hierarchy about everything in their lives. Their lives are about extremes. It is either superior or inferior, good or bad. At the top of this hierarchy is the narcissist, wielding as much power as an overlord. They can only feel safe at the top.

They must be right, be the most competent, the best and stay in control over everything. Narcissists also get the same gratification by being the worst at everything. They believe it is within their right to hurt you, and demand an apology from you in the process, so that they even things out.

- Individualism over teamwork

The concept of a team requires healthy coexistence between team members. There might be conflicts from time to time, because these are healthy and normal in a situation where people come together to exchange ideas. What's more important is understanding what other team members feel, why they feel that way, and respecting their choices.

Teamwork also requires compromise. At times you have to let someone win at your expense for the greater good. However, delayed gratification is something narcissists do not recognize. Issues like whether a given action will make everyone happy does not cross the mind of a narcissist. To them, no one else matters.

Narcissists do not have the capacity to think or be motivated by the greater good. The only thing that matters to them is their wins. They cannot give up a position, especially a strong or winning position so someone else can win. This is why such people find it easier to thrive on their own than work in groups.

- Perfectionist traits

Narcissists will go to great lengths to make sure everything is perfect. Their idea of themselves is perfect. Everyone else should be perfect. All events around them must go on as planned. Life must go according to the plan they have.

Perfection is an impossible feat to accomplish. No one is perfect so naturally, thus narcissists will be miserable and dissatisfied with life all the time. This is why they are always complaining about someone or something. Dissatisfaction is the norm in the life of a narcissist.

- Control freaks

Life is imperfect. This means constant disappointment for a narcissist. The remedy is to stay in control. Narcissists try to control everything around them. They are like puppet masters. Everything must go according to their plan. The only thing that works is that which is logical to them.

There is a script that everyone who interacts with a narcissist must follow. It is upsetting for them if you don't follow the script because it unsettles them. They want to be in control, yet you spring surprises and suddenly, they are not sure what to expect from you. Narcissists have an ideal conclusion in their minds. To achieve this, everyone must do and say what they believe is right.

In your interactions with a narcissist, you are not a person with independent feelings and thoughts. You are a character in their play. You do and say as you are told. You think as you are expected to.

- Deflection and blames

Narcissists are deeply conflicted. On one hand, they have a burning desire to stay in control. On the other hand, they must not be held accountable for results, especially if things don't go according to their plan. If things work out, then they must be recognized for the good work they have done.

Situations where things don't work out are not pleasant to narcissists. Because of this, someone else is always at fault. At times they generalize the blame on a wide spectrum, such as all teachers, all supervisors or all children. In some cases, they narrow down their blame to someone specific.

The most prolific victim in the life of a narcissist is the person they are closest to emotionally. This is usually the most loving and loyal person in their lives. It is easier to blame their flaws on you because they know you love them too much, you can never leave them, neither will you reject them. In so doing, the façade about their perfection lives to enjoy another day in the sun.

- No respect for boundaries

Where do their boundaries begin and yours end? About boundaries, there is no difference between a narcissist and a two-year-old going through the monkey see, monkey do phase. Everyone feels the way they do, wants the same things they want, and everything belongs to them. Woe unto you if you hold a contrary opinion.

Telling a narcissist no comes as a shock, and they feel deeply insulted by this. Narcissists will do everything in their power to get what they want, including pouting, rejection, demanding, persistence and cajoling.

- Invulnerability

To love someone, you must connect with them emotionally. Sharing an emotional connection means that you open your life to someone. You expose your vulnerability. You show them your weakness so they can understand you and appreciate you for the person you are, especially with your flaws. This is a deeper form of understanding that narcissists do not experience.

Narcissists cannot understand feelings. Their need for self-preservation overrides empathy (Miller & Maples, 2012). It is futile to expect them to see the world from your perspective. Emotionally, narcissists are blind. They are alone in a world where they don't understand how everyone does not see how unique they are. As a result, narcissists are emotionally needy, yet incapable of being vulnerable.

If a narcissist feels the current relationship does not satisfy their needs, it is easy for them to walk away or seek gratification by forging another relationship and overlapping the two. Someone has to feel their pain, empathize, and make things right so that they are comfortable. However, don't expect them to return the favor.

- Lack of empathy

Narcissists are self-involved, so absorbed in their lives that they cannot empathize with anyone else. It is impossible for a narcissist to feel or recognize what you feel. When interacting with a narcissist, the express expectation is that you do and feel as they do and feel. The last thing you can expect of a narcissist is an expression of guilt, remorse or apology (Saltzman, 2009)

For people who are not empathetic, narcissists have a very intense awareness of anger, rejection and perceived threats from others. They are almost blind to what people feel around them, but can misread simple gestures and facial expressions as a negative bias towards them. The closest a narcissist can come to recognizing your emotions is if you dramatically act them out.

If a narcissist is on the verge of a breakdown, saying *I love you* or *I'm sorry* could easily blow back in your face. They believe your sentiments are not genuine, and feel you are concealing an attack.

Narcissists also expect your expressions and words to align. Without this, their response is always erroneous. This explains why most narcissists read sarcasm as the truth, and jokes as personal jabs.

Apart from their inability to understand your feelings, narcissists also don't understand their own feelings, or how they form. In the mind of a narcissist, feelings are the result of actions by something or someone other than themselves. The reality of feelings being a culmination of interpretations, thoughts and complex biochemistry is something narcissists cannot embrace.

Someone else is always responsible for their feelings, especially negative feelings. It is your fault they are vulnerable, because you did not follow their plan. As a result, you are to blame. Establishing a deep connection with a narcissist is, therefore, impossible. Simply put, they are oblivious to your feelings.

- Emotional incapacitation

Reason and logic do not apply to a narcissist. This is why many times people fail when trying to explain to narcissists how their behavior affects them. The mistake that most people, especially empaths make, is to think that if the narcissist understands what you are feeling, they might change their behavior and be considerate.

None of this makes sense to a narcissist. The only thing they are aware of is what they want, their feelings and thoughts.

Occasionally, a narcissist might respond to your argument with a subtle *I understand*. However, deep down they don't.

Most decisions narcissists make are out of what they feel and how they feel about something or someone. Say they want to buy a house in an affluent neighborhood, for example. To them, they must own that house because they feel good about it, and they feel good when people know they live in an affluent neighborhood. This choice is based on what they feel, regardless of whether the purchase is a sound financial decision for the family, or for their working budget (He & Zhu, 2016).

If a narcissist is depressed, bored, wants to get into a new business, or end a relationship, they find someone or something external to address this need, instead of looking within. Their expectations come in the form of demands. If you are together, they expect you to dutifully accept their decision as the perfect solution. If you don't, you can expect waves of aggressive resentment and irritation.

- Split personalities

In the life of a narcissist, everything is either good or bad. This stems from their innate personality. From here, they split everything else especially about relationships as good or bad. A narcissist will always take credit for everything that is good or positive, but find someone to blame for all negative thoughts, actions and behavior. They deny all negative behavior and words they portray, and instead rebuke your disapproval. If they do something wrong, it is your fault they do it. You are not a good person because you don't see the good in them, and are always looking for a reason to blame them for something.

In the mind of a narcissist, the construct between good and bad can never mix. It is either horrible, bad, wonderful or good. Even in a situation that presents positive and negative outcomes, narcissists can never recognize this. In their lives, only one perspective matters – their perspective!

- Anxiety

Anxiety is a persistent feeling that something terrible is about to happen or is already happening. Most of the time anxiety is vague, because the feeling you worry about doesn't really happen. Narcissists are an anxious lot. A lot of time they speak about something they feel might happen, while some narcissists repress or find a way to hide their anxiety.

Given their predisposition for deflection, many narcissists project their anxiety to those closest to them (Ronningstam, 2012). When this happens, the victims are accused of not putting the narcissist or their needs first, being unsupportive, negative, mentally disturbed or selfish. The idea here is to goad the victim into feeling anxious, instead of the narcissist dealing with their anxiety.

As the anxiety takes a toll on you, the narcissist feels better. They grow stronger and are happy with the fact that they can control you. Sadly, if unchecked, victims who might never have shown symptoms of anxiety end up developing it, and in some cases also develop depression.

- Fear

Everything in the life of a narcissist is about fear. Fear is the motivation behind most of their decisions and actions. Many narcissists cannot identify or openly admit their fear because it is repressed and buried so deep in their subconscious, they can pretend it doesn't exist.

Narcissists are afraid of many things, honesty, real intimacy, vulnerability and so forth, because they worry that if someone gets to know them, they can identify their weaknesses and ridicule them. They are afraid of rejection, or being wrong. Some of the things narcissists are afraid of include physical or emotional abuse or attack, germs, losing their financial possessions, inadequacy, and abandonment. As a result, it is almost impossible for a narcissist to trust someone else (Huprich, Luchner, Roberts, & Pouliot, 2012)

So strong is the fear narcissists harbor that they distrust most of the people who get closer to them. They feel closeness is an attempt at gaining insider information about them, and using this to their detriment in some way. They are also afraid the more you know about them, the easier it is for you to reject, judge and abandon them when you realize they are flawed.

It is almost impossible to reassure a narcissist that the fear they harbor is unreal. While narcissists try to portray an image of self-assurance, deep down they loathe their imperfections. They are incapable of truly loving someone. When you are together, they will constantly push and test your limits with terrible behavior to see if you can break and go away. They live the life of a fraud, constantly afraid their con will be found out, and this fear never dissipates. Instead of embracing their fear and dealing with it, it is easier for them to project it on you and make you fear them.

Chapter 2: Types of Narcissists

Talks of narcissism are very common today. People throw around the word narcissist and narcissism without thinking about what it means. In fact, in modern culture, these terms have carved a life of their own, and their meanings might be slightly different from the traditional concept in psychology. Narcissism can be used as an insult today, or even a subtle dig to describe someone, especially celebrities.

Classic narcissists

Classic narcissists are identified as grandiose, exhibitionist or high-functioning narcissists. They are the basic definition of a narcissist, and the type that comes to mind whenever someone is talking about narcissism. These are people who feel too good for everyone else, yet at the same time, they still have a burning desire for everyone else to make them feel important (Casale, Fioravanti, & Rugai, 2016)

Classic narcissists are attention seekers. Most of their discussions are laced with stories about their achievements. They believe that they deserve attention and special treatment because of who they are or what they have achieved in life. Like many of their kind, most of their stories are full of half-truths.

They love to be flattered just as much as they love to flatter themselves. For a classical narcissist, a boring avenue is one where no one pays attention to them. They feel entitled and if they cannot get this for gratification, they are disappointed. A classical narcissist will also not like to share the limelight with anyone else. If they have to, they will go out of their way to make sure they do something that makes them stand out.

Vulnerable narcissists

Vulnerable narcissists also identify as a closet, victim, compensatory or fragile narcissists. This category is for narcissists who don't like attention, but still feel they are better than everyone else. Instead of seeking attention like classical narcissists, they prefer to intertwine their lives with other people (Hart, Richardson, & Tortoriello, 2018)

One of the common traits of vulnerable narcissists is to play the pity card. Their attention comes when they present themselves as wounded individuals who need to be cared for. Some vulnerable narcissists are too generous with people around them, so that you don't forget who they are, or what they did for you. What they need is admiration and attention to boost the image of their perceived worth.

Malignant narcissists

Ever heard of toxic narcissism? Well, those are malignant narcissists. Malignant narcissists are the most exploitative of the lot. They will stop at nothing to manipulate their victims into submission. A malignant narcissist is guilty of many antisocial tendencies, which might not be present in classic or vulnerable narcissists.

The simplest description of a malignant narcissist is a psychopath or a sociopath. Upon careful analysis you will realize that they are sadists, and take pleasure from their victims' pain. While the other narcissists might seek attention and approval, a malignant narcissist is always after control and domination (Trifu, 2013)

If they have to, they will be aggressive and deceitful to get their way. Anything or anyone that stands in their way will always meet their wrath. Malignant narcissists feel no pain, no remorse and are not apologetic, especially if they inflict suffering upon you in order to gain what they seek.

Overt and covert narcissists

Overt and covert narcissism is about the kind of methods the narcissist uses to get what they want. Some narcissists might be very open in their approach, while others are secretive and stealthy. Overt and covert narcissists will take advantage of someone for their personal gain (Huszcza, Berenson, & Downey, 2006). However, as their definitive names suggest, overt narcissists will be upfront about their approach. They are visible and you cannot mistake them for anything else. Their intention is clear.

Covert narcissists on the other hand are behind-the-scenes kind of people. You might not know you are under their manipulative spell until it is too late. Some covert narcissists use tactics that are so stealthy, it allows them credible cause to deny responsibility if they are caught.

Malignant narcissists have perfected the art of both overt and covert narcissism. Classical narcissists are generally overt, while vulnerable narcissists tend to be covert.

Somatic and cerebral narcissists

Somatic or cerebral narcissism is about value proposition (Y. Lee & Park, 2016). What does the narcissist see in themselves that they hold in high regard, or what do they see in someone that they want so badly? Tragically, none of these subtypes will allow their partner or anyone else to enjoy the limelight. However, they need someone around them to prop their shine. They look good, but they need someone to make them look even better.

In a relationship with such narcissists, you might assume they love to show you around, and feel special, but in a real sense what they need from you is an object they can flaunt for people to see. It gives them pleasure when people see how good you are, and praise them for making you shine. You are no more than an item in their collection.

Somatic narcissists are more attracted to their personal appearances. Their focus is on their youth, their body and what they look like. You will notice this in their selfies. You can also find many of them at the gym, and their favorite place on earth is in front of a mirror.

Cerebral narcissists believe they are the think tanks of this world. They are loaded with all kinds of information, some of which might serve no purpose. What appeals to them is the knowledge or perception that they are the most intelligent people in any gathering. A cerebral narcissist will stop at nothing to remind everyone of their accomplishments. They believe they command and demand respect because of the powerful position they have, or the powerful connections they have. Find them in any altercation and the first thing they throw at you is who they are, or the important person they can call to shut you up.

Vulnerable, malignant and classic narcissists can be either cerebral or somatic narcissists.

Inverted narcissists

Inverted narcissists are a special lot. They are covert and vulnerable in nature. They are predominantly codependent individuals. They cannot stand on their own, and always need someone to whom they can be attached.

Satisfaction and happiness for inverted narcissists come when they are connected to or are in a relationship with other narcissists. Most of their trauma can be traced back to childhood issues, like abandonment. Because they grew up in a dysfunctional system, they are more comfortable around other dysfunctional people, hence their affinity to other narcissists.

Chapter 3: Narcissistic Manipulation Techniques

Narcissists have a burning desire to be appreciated at all costs. In their minds, they are all that matters. Everyone and everything else is subordinate to their needs when it comes to gratification. While most people believe they are aware of everything that goes on around them, and are in full control, it is not always easy to deal with narcissists. Narcissists have perfected the art of manipulation.

Ideally the behavior of narcissists manifests in two ways. One set of narcissists exhibit their traits against a spectrum. It is almost impossible to predict what will trigger them. The other type of narcissists revolve around the individual's persona.

Everything is about them, their attire, possessions, fashion style and so forth. This is the type that most people are aware of.

Narcissists who expressly portray narcissistic characters are aware of the fact that they can be a lot to handle from time to time. Scientists refer to this as narcissistic awareness. On the other hand, narcissists whose tantrums manifest on a spectrum might be difficult to deal with because in their scenario, anything can trigger their outbursts.

Narcissists are exploitative, dishonest and barely show empathy. By learning about the techniques they use, you can take the first step towards learning how to loosen their manipulative grip on you, and restore your life.

The following are some of the techniques that narcissists use to pin you down:

- Gaslighting

Gaslighting is a form of psychological manipulation where the victim is manipulated into doubting their sanity, feelings or instinct (Stark, 2019). Victims end up wondering whether their version of reality is the truth or if it is distorted. Gaslighting breeds self-doubt to a point where you cannot trust yourself to think straight. You no longer feel you have a right to call out the abuser for mistreating you.

Common examples of gaslighting statements include the following phrases:

"A lot of people have been saying you are…"

"It's nothing, you are just jealous"

"That's not how it happened, are you really sure?"

Gaslighting disrupts your cognitive function, and most victims develop cognitive dissonance. You end up with two extreme beliefs about the same thing. You find yourself stuck in a position where you don't trust yourself enough to believe in what you know is right, or whether you should trust what your abuser has made you believe is the truth. In the end, you struggle with a malignant dysfunction and meeting the needs of a manipulative individual at the same time.

It is important to remind yourself what your realities are. Some victims write down things in the order they happened and review them later on. You can also talk to someone who is close to you about such events, so that they help you understand what you are going through. Gaslighting is very dangerous because if the narcissist is successful, you end up gaslighting yourself too. Distorted realities will always have a negative effect on your life. The only way to beat this is to find a way to revalidate your beliefs.

- Shaming

If you ever get into a disagreement with a narcissist, their easiest clapback is to shame you. Shaming is something that people use all the time, even those who are not narcissists. The difference is that while other people use shaming perhaps to call you out on something wrong, narcissists shame you to trim your power. If they feel you are growing stronger and out of their grip, shame makes you belittle yourself, and get back to the level they feel you deserve.

Narcissists are obsessed with their persona. They shame anyone who might be basking in the glory of their wins so your esteem can wither away. They don't do well with other people's pride. Any hint that you are making powerful strides is met with shaming statements so your self-worth diminishes and you believe in nothing but their opinion of yourself.

The venue or audience does not hold a narcissist back from shaming you. Whether you are in public or alone together, if they feel the moment is right, a narcissist will shame you by making snide comments that hurt or belittle your presence.

Malignant narcissists, for example, use your weaknesses against you. They find ways to make old wounds hurt like fresh ones, and make fresh wounds hurt worse. If they are aware of some injustice you might have experienced at some point in life, they can bring this up to stifle your growth. They say hurtful things that they believe will weaken your resolve.

- Devaluation

In a real sense, narcissists love to be worshipped. They can cultivate a culture of worship in you without your knowledge. At the beginning of your relationship, a narcissist can put you on a pedestal. In this stage, you idealize them and see nothing but good things about them. You are invested in this new relationship that everything else around you doesn't matter. As this happens, you might also cut off some of your friends because you feel they don't see you in the same light as the narcissist does. They are a burden, a bother or outright jealous that you have something beautiful, someone who adores you.

However, when you go high enough, the steady and lonely fall begins. The same things they used to build your confidence are used to destroy you. Some narcissists will hold you in high regard, but at the same time trash anyone else who might be challenging or questioning their actions.

A common example is starting a relationship with a narcissist who just broke up with someone. In the beginning, you are the best thing that ever happened in their lives. They trash their exes, and tell you how amazing you are, how different you are from everyone else. When they have had their fair share of fun, you get devalued in the same way their former partners were. Upon careful investigation, you might realize the former partner went through the same thing you are going through with their previous partner.

While relationships, especially new ones come with new experiences and sentiments of appreciation, you have to be careful and mindful of falsehoods. Even as you enjoy new love, keep your eyes open. Love bombing plays to your hormones and emotions and all sense of reason flies out the window.

- Projection

Narcissists will never see their flaws as a representation of who they are. Instead, they look for someone to hold accountable. Projection is a defense strategy which helps them make someone else responsible for their negative attributes. Instead of taking responsibility for their actions, they hold someone else in contempt.

Projection is not a trait that only narcissists experience, everyone does it at some point. However, while normal people's projection might be subtle, a narcissist's projection can be abusive psychologically and at times physically.

Narcissists have deeply rooted toxicity and shame that they cannot own up to. Instead, they project it on someone else, who ends up feeling guilty and ashamed (Metzl, 2009). In a relationship with a needy partner, instead of admitting their neediness, they can project it on you and say you are a clingy partner. This way, they don't have to deal with their problems.

Projection is essentially about shifting blame. They must come out on top all the time. In the unlikely event that things don't turn out their way, they can blame it on you or everyone else. Instead of living a happy and independent life, you are shackled to a fragile ego that you must tread carefully not to hurt.

- Baiting

Every narcissist needs a platform upon which they can practice their cruelty without reprimand. To do this, they pretend to create a sense of security. Once you are in, you are trapped. One of the techniques they use is baiting. A simple discussion soon turns into an argument which escalates into chaos with someone who seems to have no idea about respect. Initially, you might respond to the subtle argument politely, but the real intention was to wreak havoc.

Narcissists take time to learn about you. They know what your insecurities are, words that trigger your emotions and so forth. They know topics that are dear to you, things in your past that you feel strongly about, which might provoke you. These are the things they target. This is how you are baited.

Once you fall for the trick and hit rock bottom, they take a step back and pretend to care. They ask if you are okay, and insist they had no intention of agitating you. All this is fake, but because you are already worked up, you take the apology and believe their words. This will happen repeatedly until you realize the pattern and notice the malice behind it.

- Control

Toxic narcissists and abusers always strive to stay in control. They feel good when things are going according to plan. They must control everyone and everything in their environment.

In a relationship, a narcissist will try to alienate you from your social circles. They will talk about how your family and friends are a bad influence on you, and that you should cut them off. Once you are isolated and they have you wrapped around their finger, they can do with you as they please. Every aspect of your life is under their control, from your social networks (online and offline) to finances. They must be briefed on everything you do, or you might be banned from engaging anyone else. Some victims are locked away from the rest of the world as a form of punishment.

Narcissists find it very easy to conjure conflicts whenever they feel their victim is enjoying *too much freedom*. The idea here is to make you lose your balance, feel vulnerable and follow their instructions. This is the reason why they create frivolous arguments about petty issues.

During a moment of calm, they appear relaxed, but in a real sense, they are watching you and waiting for a moment when you feel you are gaining control, so they can push you back into the abyss. Interacting with a narcissist means oscillating between their real self and the fake persona. As a result, it is impossible for you to read a narcissist's mind. You don't know their true identity. If you are in an emotional relationship, it can be frightening because they change all of a sudden, and you have no idea what happened to the person you fell in love with.

For a victim, such control is dangerous because as the narcissist gains more control over your emotions and your life, you lose faith and belief in yourself. You get to a point where you recondition your mind to believe their falsehoods as the truth. Your self-esteem goes down the drain. You normalize the abuse and embrace it as your new reality.

- Generalizations

Some narcissists are very lazy at their own game. Instead of carefully studying a situation and determining how to respond amicably, they generalize with a blanket statement that ignores all elements of the discourse. If you have a differing opinion, it is easier for them to relegate your opinion into a general label.

Why do narcissists generalize everything? Their concept of generalization is as a result of an insane stereotype and schema about society. They have predominant assumptions which must align with their expectations. It is almost impossible to rationalize an argument with such a narcissist because they see everything as a subtle attack on their personality.

In a personal relationship, confronting a narcissist about something will result in a generalization about yourself. It is common to get feedback like *"You never appreciate what I do for you"* or *"You are always overreacting."* While it is true that you might overreact from time to time, most of the time it is the abuser trying to get into your head and turn their flaws into your problem.

- Patronization

One of the traits that narcissists portray is to constantly degrade someone. Their idea of sarcasm is often a condescending statement. While everyone else can use sarcasm for fun, narcissists use sarcasm as a manipulative tool so that the victim feels degraded and patronized (Belikova & Sue-Chan, 2015). While their statements will hurt you, they don't expect you to react negatively. If you do, you are misconstrued as too sensitive, and they may say you need to lighten up a bit.

What is interesting about this predicament is that narcissists are usually the temperamental ones, and every time you rationalize something with them, they retort that you are being too sensitive. As this persists, the victim adapts and learns how to cope with the situation.

Over time you learn to be vigilant about voicing your opinion without being reprimanded. In so doing, the narcissist succeeds in hurting you with very little effort. Self-censorship is a sign that the narcissist is winning, because you learn how to shut yourself down even before they do.

- Pushing boundaries

Narcissists will always push your boundaries to see what you can do, and to identify your limits. They try to cross as many of your boundaries as possible without consequences. Each time they do this, their resolve grows stronger. This also explains why survivors of emotional and physical abuse who reconcile with, and go back to their abusers usually suffer worse damage than the previous incidents.

Narcissists and other abusers pretend to be remorseful. They lure you back with empty promises that they will change. Some might even join a program that should help them change. However, once they have you where they want you, everything changes and your suffering intensifies. In their minds, pushing your limits is the perfect punishment you deserve for standing up against their abuse, and more importantly, for coming back. They believe you came back because the previous incidents were not enough. They have to take things a notch higher so you can feel real pain, pain enough for you not to return.

- Shifting goal posts

There is a very thin line between destructive and constructive criticism. Destructive criticisms are laced with unattainable standards and personal attacks. Narcissists have perfected destructive criticism. Instead of helping you improve, their goal is to pin you down and use you as their pink slip out of any situation. By shifting goal posts, you can never win with a narcissist. They have an ace up their sleeves for every move you make.

Shifting goal posts is another way for narcissists to show everyone how dissatisfied they are with you in all aspects. You might be armed with proof and valid facts showing your capability, but each time they will put up roadblocks in your path, demanding that you go the extra mile.

Say your career is successful and you are content with what you have achieved so far, a narcissist will respond to this by asking you why you are not driving luxury cars yet. Most of their goal posts are unrelated. The ultimate goal is to have you confused, and in this state, you have to do all you can to get their validation and approval.

Each time someone raises the bar too high for you especially after you have gone out of your way to prove you are worthy, it distorts your balance. You feel unworthy, unaccomplished and undeserving of anything good. Instead of praising you for what you have achieved against all the odds, they focus on a tiny element that takes away the shine from your success. In the long run, you lose your ground and devote your life to satisfying their unending and unachievable need for gratification. Unfortunately, this takes your focus away from the abuse you endure in their hands.

- Accountability

One of the tactics narcissists love to use is to change the subject and divert attention to themselves. They do this to escape accountability. A narcissist must never be held accountable for anything. If such a discussion is going on, it serves their interests well if they divert attention to something else, something that suits them.

In therapy, a victim of narcissistic abuse might mention a period of neglect that hurt them emotionally. Instead of listening, the narcissist will cut in by mentioning a mistake that the victim committed a week ago. Each time you try to hold them accountable, they find a reason to divert attention from that situation by identifying something to blame you for, in an attempt to prove that you deserve what you got.

- Threats

Narcissists will create impossible expectations and challenging obstacles in your life just so they can punish you for failing to live up to expectations. Most arguments with narcissists are futile. From the very beginning, you are destined to fail. The fact that you tried will be used against you.

Instead of engaging in a healthy disagreement or argument in a mature manner, narcissists will try to highlight the consequences of failing to comply. Even as you participate in what you think is an honest and mature discourse, at the back of your mind you cannot ignore the lingering threat.

Most discussions and arguments with narcissists are laced with ultimatums. *Either, or* statements are the norm. They can threaten you overtly or covertly, and as long as you are cowed into submission, their message is home.

- Name-calling

No one builds a mountain out of an anthill faster than a narcissist. Anything that they feel is an attack on their perceived superiority is a threat that must be dealt with swiftly. The narcissist is always right. Anyone who challenges this will feel the wrath of their narcissistic rage. This rage is not necessarily out of low self-esteem, but a false sense of power and entitlement.

If a narcissist cannot find something to manipulate you into acting or thinking the way they want you to, name-calling is always a reliable weapon. Name-calling is aimed at degrading you. Some of the names narcissists call you in this moment of rage are so hurtful, they attack your behavior, appearance and intelligence. They remind you that you don't deserve to have an independent opinion. Your right to it is insignificant, if not invalid.

Name-calling targets your insights, opinions and beliefs. Core beliefs, for example, are the core of your personality. These are ideas that have defined your life and shaped you into the amazing person you are. When someone attacks your core beliefs, they are attacking the very foundation of your being, your personality. They are attacking you as an individual and goading you to change into someone else. Instead of responding to an argument with facts, narcissists come after you. Your intelligence and credibility mean nothing to them.

- Defensiveness

Be careful about people who insist on how good they are and that you should trust them because everyone does. Trust is a tricky affair. It is earned. In a relationship, it is something you earn from the simple things someone does when you are around them. Someone can do something subtle and unrelated to you, but in that moment, it evokes a feeling and you feel comfortable around them, and trust them.

Narcissists and other abusers will do so much to prove that they are compassionate, kind and trustworthy. You should worry when someone you just met insists that you should trust them. Why are they imposing their trust on you? Before you can trust them, what makes them think they should trust you in the first place?

Trust is built around a stable foundation. Toxic narcissists are capable of creating a false sense of empathy and sympathy around you especially at the beginning of your relationship. All this is a careful attempt at confusing you to let your guard down. By the time you realize the mistake you made, you are so deep in their snare you can't find a way out.

Genuine people don't have to advertise their niceness. They exude positivity around them. You can see it in the way they interact with people and how people speak about them. Some things come naturally to people. Trust is earned through reciprocation, not a rehearsal. If you meet someone who is constantly highlighting the good things about themselves, take a step back.

- Triangulation

Triangulation is a situation where the abuser introduces another person's perspective or opinion into your relationship dynamic, with the sole purpose of validating their abuse towards you, and invalidating your reaction to it (Wright & Furnham, 2015). Bringing in a third party always has disastrous effects. In most cases, triangulation breeds love triangles, and by the time you realize what's going on, you are too insecure and unhinged.

Triangulation is a common trait in malignant narcissists. They introduce, family members, friends, former partners, workmates or even strangers into the picture to make you jealous and create an air of uncertainty around you. Each time they need their perspective validated, they use someone else.

It is one of the best diversionary tactics narcissists use because you end up thinking that if someone else, a stranger to your relationship sees things differently, then probably your perspective is flawed. Your attention moves away from their abuse to a faux belief that they are right, highly sought after and desirable. Instead of addressing your abuse, you question yourself. If someone else agrees with them, then the only sensible option is that you are wrong.

A narcissist will come to you with tales of bad things people say about you. However, what you don't realize is that no one is saying bad things about you, they are.

Part II: Narcissism In Relationships

Chapter 4: How to Handle a Narcissistic Partner

One of the most difficult things for victims of narcissists is learning to let go. When someone is dear to you, it is normal to see the best in them. You try to get them help, try to understand them and hope that someday they will change. Unfortunately, this is not always the case.

Narcissists do not seek help. They believe they don't have a problem. If anything, in the mind of a narcissist, the person who thinks they need to change their ways is the one who needs to embrace change. It is so traumatizing, watching someone you love dive deeper into the abyss like that.

If you cannot change someone, at best you can learn how to cope with them. Remember that in as much as you might hold them dear, your first priority is your personal safety and peace of mind. In learning how to handle a narcissist, you can counter their manipulative motives and prevent yourself from becoming a puppet.

The first step is to learn how to identify a narcissist, which we have done. Next, you learn how to identify their manipulative traits, and what to do in order to counter their outbursts. In a relationship, it is very difficult when you realize you are living with a narcissist. The best solution is always to keep a healthy distance from a narcissist, especially if you know they can overpower your resolve.

Four-point framework for dealing with a narcissist

There are several ways of handling a narcissist. Before we look into them, the following are four of the most important things you should always keep in mind when dealing with a narcissist.

1. Positivity

Life throws many curve balls at you all the time. It never gets easier. To get through anything, you must embrace positivity and change your outlook about life. Narcissists will drain the life out of you, and by the time they are done with you, all that's left might be a shell of your former self.

People who maintain a positive approach to life generally live happier lives than most. Your happiness is one of the things a narcissist will go after. When you are happy, to them it means there is something else in your life responsible for your happiness, something other than them. Since your life must revolve around them, they will do everything they can to take away your happiness.

Narcissists will do random things to disturb your peace. They also monitor you to see the effect. It fills them with joy when you lose focus and are disturbed. They respond by pushing your limits further until you break.

Staying positive will help you learn how to handle a narcissist. They have an endless barrage of insults and ill behavior that they can hurl at you. Instead of bowing to the pressure, be positive and show them that you are not affected by the things they do or what they say. If you are persistent, they might soon realize that it is impossible to break you, and they have to make peace with it.

Positivity is not just about handling a narcissist, it is also about your mindset. You need to stay sharp because a narcissist will never give up on testing you. You can condition your mind to think positively, filter negative vibes and focus only on things that bring joy, meaning and satisfaction in your life. This will help you become aware of, and impervious to narcissistic manipulation.

2. Healthy boundaries

One of the top recommendations when dealing with a narcissist is to set boundaries. This helps, especially when you realize you are in an unhealthy relationship. The challenge with setting boundaries is that in most cases, people don't even know what their boundaries are. It is very difficult to change something you don't know you have.

Setting boundaries depends on your previous experiences and upbringing. It might be easier for some people to establish boundaries than others because of such predispositions. It might take some learning, but if you are persistent, you will get it right.

First, you need to learn what you are about. What are your boundaries? You must acknowledge your feelings. Boundaries are only effective when you know what you are protecting, hence what you are shielding yourself from (Newland, 2008). Does someone's comment make you feel terrible? Do you feel drained when you are in their presence? This is a good place to start.

Learning about yourself helps you evaluate your actions and choices, and recognize how you feel. Most people have leaky boundaries in their relationships, and at some point they give up altogether. In such a relationship, you become so engrossed in your partner's life that you substitute your life for theirs. Relationships are about two unique individuals coming together to form a healthy unit.

Take some time to rethink your life. Reflect and check in with yourself until you are aware of the difference between your partner or the other party to this interaction, and yourself.

Second, how do you know when your boundaries are crossed? Once you are aware of your feelings, you know when you are hurt. That is the point your boundaries are breached. Ask yourself how was your boundary breached? Here are some examples.

Scenario 1:

"Your partner always promises to take you out and meet their friends and family, but it never happens."

Scenario 2:

"Someone in your life is always asking for money, promising to pay back but they never do."

Scenario 3:

"A close friend or family member keeps calling you in the middle of the night or messaging about their problems, but they don't seem interested in solving the problems themselves. Each time they call, you cannot fall asleep after the call."

Each time these events happen, something breaks inside you. You feel disappointed, unloved, cheated, unappreciated and so forth. You already know what matters to you, and how you feel when those feelings are not appreciated. Now, you know how your boundaries are breached.

Third, you focus on how to reset boundaries. You are in charge of your life, and to borrow a common phrase in many establishments, *Management reserves the right of admission*!

Why should you put up with someone who has made it clear they don't respect anything you say? Having realized the things that hurt you and how, the next step is to confront the problem. Address the person who keeps breaching your boundaries without a care.

Here are some examples on how to handle the scenarios above:

Scenario 1

Tell your partner why it bothers you that they haven't kept this promise. Tell them to stop making the promise altogether, and act on it once and get it out of the way.

Scenario 2

Remind them that since they have failed to honor their commitments, you will not lend them more money until they pay back what they owe.

Scenario 3

Tell your friend or family member that you understand their pain, but it is draining the life out of you. Ask them to seek professional help, and if possible, stop answering the calls.

By addressing these issues, you make the other person aware that they are hurting you, and they need to stop.

Fourth, you must learn how to ground your boundaries. Establishing boundaries is one thing, but maintaining them is not easy either. If you have weak boundaries, your partner will recognize this and can manipulate you into feeling guilty through backlash. However, the most important thing is that these boundaries are there for you.

You must respect your boundaries before you expect the same of someone else. Grounding your boundaries is more about awareness and strengthening your resolve. Meditation, deep breathing, chakra are some of the techniques you can use to enforce your boundaries.

While enforcing your boundaries, don't forget your emotions. They are valid. Trust in yourself. You are not wrong to set your boundaries. This is healthy, and everyone must respect each other's boundaries if you are to be happy together. You have individual boundaries and couple boundaries. Each of these boundaries are unique, and it is their independence that makes your relationship healthy.

Fifth, talk about your boundaries. Talk about it. Let your partner know you have boundaries and they have persistently crossed them, and you need them to stop. Fair warning, this might not always go well. If your partner retorts, argues back or lashes out at you for having boundaries, perhaps it is best you walk away and take care of yourself. It is clear that you are not a priority to them.

Backlash is usually one of the signs that someone does not acknowledge or respect your boundaries. Arguing with them about it is an acknowledgement of their disrespect, which opens room for unhealthy compromise. Boundaries are simple. If someone doesn't understand them, the best they can do is ask you to enlighten them about your boundaries and need thereof. This can help them understand you better, and why you need the boundaries.

Boundaries must come with consequences. People will always push your boundaries, at times just to see what happens. Decide on appropriate consequences and communicate them clearly. Setting consequences is the ultimate way of embracing your boundaries. Make this about you. After all, the purpose of boundaries is to honor your commitment to your inner peace, not to judge or satisfy another person's choices and actions.

Finally, take care of yourself. If the discussion about your boundaries did not go according to plan, don't spend your time worrying about it. Step outside, exercise, run along the beach, go for a walk or something. Do anything that will prevent you from spending a lot of your energy worrying about what transpired earlier.

3. Personal detachment

Narcissists will always project their flaws to you. They blame you for things that you have nothing to do with. They will undermine you and break your spirit. A good solution for this is to retreat and embrace a different approach so that you learn how to deal with their tirades.

Learn how to ignore their personal attacks. Don't take anything a narcissist says personally. When you do this, it is easier for you to handle the situation better. The last thing you want to do is pick up an argument with a narcissist because they will never listen to you. At best, let them know you don't agree with their position, and leave it at that.

Any encounter with a narcissist is most likely about them, and never about you. In order to identify and reject these attacks, you should understand your self-worth, believe in yourself, and shun any criticism that they might level against you.

4. Contextual evaluation

What is the situation at hand? Take time and learn the context before you respond to a narcissist. Some of their outbursts are not because they are narcissists but because of circumstances which eventually make them embrace the narcissistic personality.

A good example is when you are offered a promotion over your colleague who has a narcissistic personality, and was eyeing the position too. Working together might not be easy. Your colleague will easily resent you for no reason. They will highlight your mistakes and wonder how you got the job instead of them.

Even if your colleague is not usually a confronting person, they might develop a condescending attitude towards you. In any argument or disagreement, they will throw words like "*so you think you are better than everyone else,*" to vent and air out their frustration. It is always wise to assess the context of these tirades so that you know what you are dealing with and why.

Tips for dealing with a narcissist

A lot of things might run through your mind when you encounter a narcissist. It is normal that you might be engulfed by the desire to flee the situation. While self-preservation is important, you should also have it at the back of your mind that narcissistic personality disorder is a real mental problem, and if possible, encourage the individual to seek medical attention.

Besides those who have NPD, there are individuals who portray narcissistic characteristics. It is quite helpful if you know how to handle such people. This helps in managing your expectations, and creating a safe environment for you to interact with them without their narcissistic tendencies taking over. Below are useful ideas that will help you manage the situation better:

- Acceptance

One of the first things you have to do is realize that this person is who they are. Accept them. There is no version of themselves that you can create in your mind that will change their behavior. Many victims of narcissistic abuse suffer because deep down they hold onto a fallacy that someday, the abuser might change their ways. The only thing that might happen is your life changing for the worst.

- Deny them attention

Narcissists are attention hogs. Since they thrive on attention, why not shut them out? These are people who will do anything to be recognized. The attention might be positive or negative, but they will still thrive off of it. If you give them all the attention they need, the only thing that happens is that you end up sacrificing what is important to you, to satisfy them. Attention seekers like these will never respect you. They never see you in the same way you see them.

- Establish boundaries

The trick is not just establishing boundaries, but creating very clear boundaries. Communicate. Talk to the other person about what you feel when they do something that exceeds your boundaries. Set consequences and make sure they are aware of what it will cost them the next time they cross your boundaries.

More importantly, hold them accountable for their actions. You have to be steadfast in your approach to dealing with narcissists. A narcissist will try to find the easiest way to get back control from you. While you set these boundaries, they might feel you are moving further away from them, which is infuriating. Instead, ensure you communicate the boundaries to them in a healthy way. Do it in a manner that does not feel like they are being attacked.

There are sacrifices you can make for people who are dear to you, like these ones. However, at the same time you must also be aware that some people might never change. If this is that kind of a person, then your personal safety and peace of mind comes first, and the best thing to do is to walk away. It does not matter if they are your parents, siblings or lovers; walking away might be the only way you stay alive.

- Retaliation

When you figure out how to handle a narcissist, do not assume they will take it kindly. Expect retaliation. Some mind tricks might be coming your way, so brace yourself for impact. One of the common responses to your boundaries is that they will also give you a list of their boundaries or demands. Be careful because what might seem like a counter offer to your boundaries might be a manipulation tactic.

It is common for a narcissist to state their terms in such a way that you feel guilty about your boundaries. They need you to go back to the drawing board and rethink your strategy. They can even make you feel like you are pushing them away. If you fall for this trick, you give up control of your life. Watch out for the sympathetic pleas, because in most cases, they are anything but sympathetic.

- Stand your ground

The last thing you can expect from a narcissist is that they will admit they made a mistake, or take responsibility for hurting you. Instead of owning up to it, it is easier for them to make you bear the responsibility for their actions. This is why you must always stand your ground. Be strong in your resolve because you know what is right. Do not give in to the manipulation. Theirs is an inflated ego that you can never truly please. Accepting the blame will only create more trouble for you in the future.

- No promises

You might have learned this about your partner already, their promises never materialize. You cannot keep up that unhealthy cycle. Instead of worrying about what happens next, insist on immediate action. If they promise you something, make sure they do it right away. Hold them accountable for it and insist on action.

The reason why you need to do this is because most of the time, promises from narcissists are nothing but a means to an end. Whenever they make a promise, there is something they want from you. Once they have it, the promises become a distant memory.

Chapter 5: Effects of Narcissism in Relationships

You know you shouldn't fall in love with a narcissist, but somehow, you find yourself entangled in a toxic relationship with one. How did you end up here? After all, narcissists love no one else above themselves. You are looking for someone to love and cherish you as much as you love and cherish them, yet you end up with someone who is incapable of loving you, or even recognizing you beyond a glance.

Why do we fall in love with narcissists? What is it about them, or ourselves that makes this supposedly impossible connection possible? Someone who is too engrossed in their ideology of themselves should fundamentally be unattractive, yet here we are.

We live in a world where fantasy has been glorified, and everyone keeps chasing after something unreal at some point.

At the back of your mind, you know what you seek, or what is before you is superficial, a smoke screen, yet the allure of attaining the impossible is too strong, so you yield.

Take speed dating, for example. Many people have participated in one or more. How do you get to know someone by summarizing highlights of their life? Speed dating is one of the lamest things in as far as relationships are concerned, yet many people throng the venues in the hope that they can find someone to settle with.

In such a case, who is at fault? Is it the narcissist who presents their case as a well-to-do, accomplished, person of your dreams kind of partner, or the seeker, who is impressed by, and accepts nothing short of what the narcissist says they are? However, speed dating is not our concern, but an attempt at highlighting how complicated relationships can be, especially in terms of needs assessment (Houser, Horan, & Furler, 2008)

Narcissists are desperate, not just for attention, but also for self-love. They need to constantly convince themselves that they are good enough. If they are good enough for themselves, they have to be good enough for you too. This is one of the reasons why rejection doesn't always work well for a narcissist. It is not easy for them to reconcile it in their minds that someone thinks and feels they are not good enough.

While narcissists are at fault for their grandiose perception of themselves, at times you have to look inwards to understand your role in some unfortunate events. For the record, this is not to blame the victim, but to help you see things from a different perspective. Narcissists might be held accountable for manipulating you into a relationship, but you can get out. You deserve to be happy, and you deserve a happy and healthy relationship. Earlier on we saw some of the defining characteristics and manipulative traits of narcissists. This helped us understand who they are, how to identify them, and why they behave the way they do. In this section, we will try to understand you, the victim, and how narcissism is perpetuated in your life.

Why am I attracting narcissists?

Ever felt like you are a narcissist magnet? Somehow, you keep ending up in relationships with narcissists, and this is not just about personal relationships, but the whole spectrum, including professional relations. While you might worry about attracting narcissists, this is not the main problem. The real problem is that you are holding onto them.

Let's try an exercise. Answer the following questions about your interactions and relationships truthfully:

Do you have defined boundaries about behavior and attitudes you can tolerate from your partner?

Would you end a relationship because your partner is selfish and doesn't consider your needs?

How do you handle an abusive relationship? Walk away or stay and hope your partner will change?

Do you excuse ill behavior from your partner, and make excuses for them?

These might seem like mundane things but they form the platform upon which a narcissistic partner will get away with devaluing you and your opinion all the time.

Here are some reasons why you might find yourself in a relationship with a narcissist, an abusive relationship you struggle to get out of:

- Caregiving spirit

Caregiving is a good deed. You empathize with someone who lacks, and out of the kindness of your heart, you take care of them. Many high achievers in society are in relationships with narcissists, some without knowing it. As a high achiever, you know you can take care of yourself. As a result, you always turn down the chance for someone to take care of you. You offer to pay for meals and drinks all the time. There is nothing wrong with taking care of yourself. However, to compensate for this lack of vulnerability, it is easier for you to take care of others. In so doing, you end up attracting people who constantly need help.

- You fall for the name-dropping charm

Everyone knows someone important. When it comes to celebrity stories, everyone has something that can light up a conversation. Whether it is true or another story they heard from someone else, they tell their tales so vividly you can almost live in the moment through their words.

"Oh, you know Vettel too? He's such a nice person. He's friends with one of my buddies at work, we hang out from time to time."

If this kind of thing works for you, there is a good chance you will never see beyond a narcissist's name-dropping charm. Their stories and encounters are full of big names. It gets worse when they realize this appeals to you. They do this in a bid to conceal their insecurities about themselves and instead, lavish you with the idea of this glamorous life they live. Be warned, however, this charm is ingenuine. It is a ploy to seek and maintain attention. After all, who doesn't want to hear more about how to sneak into Buckingham Palace?

- Flattery is your undoing

Flattery can make you feel so good, but it doesn't last. At best, it can get you in a good mood. Narcissists crave attention.

Nothing stands in their way when they want it. The use of flattery works for them because they can flatter you to get your attention, then immediately go on about themselves.

Flattery for a narcissist is not necessarily about needing compliments. In some cases, it is about paranoia, as the narcissist goes through their regular attention-seeking routine, and to boost their fragile ego.

- Hovering for a second chance

If you are in a relationship with a narcissist and you break up with them, please let them go. Don't hold on, hoping that they might change and come back better. Narcissists love to hover around in the aftermath of a breakup. They had all your attention, which they don't enjoy anymore. This makes them feel helpless and abandoned, in which case the only alternative is to lure you back by any means necessary.

There are several tricks that they can use for this, including making a half-hearted apology, convincing you that they will not do what made you break up again and so forth. Some will even send you photos of themselves looking sad. All this is to guilt you into taking them back.

Remember that you let them go because they disrespected you, and you felt that they cannot change. Such a person cannot change in a few days. They can, however, learn how to camouflage their real intent. Most people who take their narcissistic partners back usually suffer more pain and emotional trauma than they did earlier on.

- You sustain the drama

Narcissists get bolder over time. They come at your boundaries, hoping you will cave and get softer with them. Your life with them is full of so much drama, you can't seem to catch a break. Netflix would be jealous of your life. Think about this for a moment: how peaceful is your life when your narcissist partner is out of town for work, or when they have traveled for some other reason?

When you are all alone, things are easy, smooth, peaceful, until they come back and all the upheaval starts. A narcissist will always leave you devoid of energy. All their demands will leave you worn, drained and exhausted. All you ever do is provide for everything they need, from attention to affection. At the beginning of your relationship, this might feel okay, because perhaps you are trying to impress them or keep up with their energy. However, after a while you realize you cannot keep up, and you are demoralized after an encounter with them.

- You are a hopeless empath

If there is one category that narcissists love, and are surprisingly more drawn to them it has to be empaths. Life can be very cruel and unfair. Why do such nice, loving and caring people end up with partners who leave them more worn out than confidential documents having passed through a paper shredder?

The secret lies in your personality. As an empath, you are an understanding person. You believe that everyone deserves a chance. You see the good in everyone, even when you shouldn't. You believe that given time, you can turn a bad person into a good person. If you spend enough time with them, you can show them the goodness of their hearts, and make them change and embrace a new life (Stadler, 2017). This is where you go wrong, and open your life to toxicity.

Narcissists are wounded animals. As an empath, you want to take care of them. They know this better than you do. They know you are naturally inclined to try and fix them. When you meet, they will talk about how rough life has been for them in the past, perhaps in relationships, or their work or anything else that draws your sympathy. While it is okay to be kind, you must be very careful about who you show your kindness to.

Why empaths attract narcissists

The attraction between an empath and a narcissist is one of those instinctive connections that just happen. You feel like you were meant to be together. You clicked the very first time you met and it seems you have found the right person for you, until you wake up from the bad dream that has been months or years of your life. What's unfortunate for most empaths is that they will often end up in another relationship with another narcissist.

Narcissist-empath relationships are very toxic. You are exposed to so much pain that people who were once close to you can barely recognize you. Narcissists and empaths share some attributes that are attractive to one another, which is one of the reasons why they always seem destined to meet one another.

For the empath, however, it is nothing but bad news. All your goodness will be misconstrued for weakness, and exploited by a narcissistic partner. In order to understand why this relationship happens in the first place, here are some reasons why you are drawn together:

- You are a natural healer

A narcissist will always appeal to an empath because you have natural healer tendencies. There is something so nurturing about you. Everyone knows it and it shows. You are a natural healer because you are sensitive. You are sensitive to people's feelings and needs. Because of your sensitivity, you will not just recognize their vulnerability, but you will understand it (Freedy, 2016).

Empaths go beyond understanding narcissists' pain. You want to empower them to become better. You want to share their pain so they don't feel all alone. This triggers something in the mind of a narcissist. No one has shown them this much attention and affection before. It makes them feel special, and they know you are the one they have been looking for.

Your sensitivity to their pain, or supposed pain is genuine, but everything else about them is not. However, because of your sensitivity, you become entangled because you are both getting emotional satisfaction. It gets even worse if you have a lot of things in common other than the emotional connection. This gives you a chance to see them all the time, while it gives them a chance to hog your space all the time.

The problem here is that because of the emotional connection you share, what might have been short-term gratification is easily advanced to something else, something bigger than it was supposed to be in the first place. By the time they go full narcissist on you in the relationship, you are so confused you can't understand why this is happening to you, and you might even feel responsible for your predicament.

Being an empath, you remind yourself that you knew they were wounded when you met them. You remember the good times and how amazing life was. You question your role in why they turned into the animal you live with, and believe that you are at fault for all the pain you are going through. You blame yourself for your pain and their pain and convince yourself you are not a worthy partner, and deserve to be treated as you are.

- You are easy to manipulate

Narcissists are natural manipulators. Nothing comes easier to a narcissist than this. On the other hand, you listen. An empath heals, loves, cares for people and more importantly, forgives them – everything a narcissist craves.

Each time your partner abuses you, you see beyond the pain and abuse, you see a work in progress. You see someone who can become something better. You believe that one day they will come full circle and be the person you believe they should be.

Each time you are hurt, you forgive them because forgiveness comes naturally to you. However, on their part, this shows how weak you are. They have more control and power over you. In the end, you both get what you want. You feel you are helping them by empathizing, while on their part, they feel emboldened and stronger then they have you where they want you.

Your empathy masks something deeper: doubt in yourself. You can only overlook your pain for so long. You feel you are in a healthy relationship. Whenever you talk to someone about your relationship, you convince yourself that every relationship has its problems. None of them is perfect. You believe your relationship will endure and stand the test of time.

- They need help

Narcissists have different characteristics. Everyone who has encountered one will describe them according to their experience. One thing that stands out in most of them is that they need help. They always present themselves as victims of sustained abuse and trauma, which they somehow overcame to get to the place they are in life.

For an empath, you see a story of struggle, someone who has overcome all obstacles and succeeded against all the odds. You are naturally drawn not to the person, but to their struggle. You feel life never dealt them a good hand, so you can change that. You can make their load lighter.

A narcissist might complete their story with a boost of confidence, to prove to you that they are strong. Deep down, however, they feel worthless. You are mistaken to offer them your sympathy. What they need from you is validation. As an empathy, validation comes naturally because you feel they deserve the kindness, when in real sense it is not the kindness they seek.

Opening up to you about their struggle makes you believe they are vulnerable, and this is where the attraction happens. Remember that you cannot fix someone. People change because they have a reason to. People change for the better because they understand why they are changing. They change because they have something valuable in their life that they risk losing if they stay as they are. A narcissist does not value you, they value themselves. Change is a fallacy.

In conclusion, a narcissist and an empath might look like two people destined for a great relationship at the beginning, but it can only end in pain. Empaths are givers, while narcissists are takers. A narcissist will go out of their way to impress you and shower you with a lavish lifestyle. Your engagement ring alone will be the talk of your peers for generations to come. However, for every single thing a narcissist gives, they take back tenfold. They shower you with material possessions to mask the priceless emotional wealth they steal from you. As you build towards a healthy, happy and successful future, understanding the differences between yourself and a narcissistic partner will help you make the right decision.

Part III: Surviving Narcissistic Abuse

Chapter 6: Psychological Violence on Victims of Narcissistic Abuse

Psychological violence is a form of violence where the victim is exposed to psychological trauma. One of the challenges with psychological violence is that unlike physical violence, there might not be physical scars as evidence. Psychological violence happens each time the victim is subjected to emotional distress. In many cases, psychological violence is accompanied by verbal or physical violence.

Many people are victims of psychological violence at some point in time, but they are never aware of it. Without proper understanding of yourself, and what your life is about, you might never know when you are under attack. It also becomes difficult to come up with effective strategies you can use to cope with the trauma from such abuse.

While anyone is susceptible to this kind of abuse, women and children are the most affected by psychological abuse. The attacks target perceptions, feelings and thoughts. Psychological abuse might not be physical, but the effect on the victim's persona is just as bad.

In a relationship with a narcissistic partner, there are several symptoms, reactions and conditions that the victim might experience which are a sign of abuse. The narcissist conditions the victim by creating experiences in relationships which have a negative impact on the victim. Here are some of the signs you might be suffering psychological abuse in your relationship:

- **Intense insecurities** – your abuser identifies your personal insecurities and over time, uses them to put you down. Your insecurities grow stronger and you cannot trust anyone.

- **Disbelief in yourself** – many victims' lives change for the worse because they no longer believe in themselves. Your confidence is eroded to a point where you can no longer trust your judgement.

- **Incapability** – victims of abuse who were once assured

and competent in everything they do suddenly become incapable and uncertain about everything.

- **Anxiety** – you live a life of uncertainty and fear. You are constantly afraid something bad will happen. You don't trust good things because you believe the happiness is short-lived and will turn for the worst soon after. You also feel emotionally drained and incapable of enjoying true happiness.

- **Indecision** – victims who were once grounded become indecisive, confused and unable to trust anyone, not even themselves.

- **Esteem issues** – psychological abuse erodes your confidence. You cannot see yourself as anything better than what your abuser says you are. You shy away from the public, afraid that everyone sees the weaknesses in you.

These are the effects of psychological abuse. They manifest in different ways, but one thing is certain about them – they erode the very core of your being, your personality. If you cannot recognize yourself, how can someone else?

Psychological violence by narcissists is meted out to victims in different categories. We will address five of the spheres of life where healthy relationships are important, and how narcissists take everything away from you.

Children and Families

- Trust issues

Life is one big frightening place for a child raised by narcissists. Strings are attached to everything, especially love. Children need unconditional love, however, children of narcissistic parents grow up learning that there is always something attached to it. Such children grow up suspicious of affection. It becomes difficult for them to trust anyone, especially those who are getting too close to them (Keene & Epps, 2016).

Interestingly enough, while such children struggle to embrace genuine affection, they are drawn to toxic relationships and affection. This happens because the feelings shared in such relationships are those that are too familiar, they can relate. Toxic relationships become a comfortable place for such children.

It is easier for a child brought up in a narcissistic environment to trust a bad person disguised as their savior than it is for them to trust someone who is genuine and offers emotional stability.

Toxic people are an embodiment of the same challenges the children endured when growing up. Because their minds have been conditioned to embrace such instances, they are not afraid to interact with toxic people. They learn not to trust, or not to trust too much – this is easier because they have done it all their life.

- Inability to commit

Children raised in a narcissistic environment struggle with commitment issues. When you meet them, at first glance they seem like they are looking to establish commitment with someone. However, deep down they fear commitment. These kids grow up alienated by the people closest to them, so it is difficult to commit to someone or something. Commitment for such children is often on the basis of what feels right at the moment, not because they really want to commit.

Long-term relationships are not easy to get into because the feeling of being tied down to something is odd. When they encounter someone who loves them truly, it is unsettling because they have to open up about their vulnerabilities to this person, and they are not sure whether this person will stay or walk away. When you grow up alienated by family, stability and forever relationships become a fallacy to you.

Commitment to someone for such a child means that they are giving up control of their lives. Someone else is in charge of their emotions. Naturally, such children will go into defense mode to protect themselves from being hurt. They know the feeling, they have lived through it, and cannot risk it again. When facing the prospect of an intense relationship, it is easier to withdraw, even without a reason. They find it easier to give up on someone who loves them and push them away, than be with them and experience unconditional love.

- Hyperactive attunement

Hyperactivity is one of the symptoms victims of abuse learn to help them cope with their abuser. It helps them know when things are about to get messy. They are keen to subtle changes in the way the abuser responds to them. This makes them realize changes in facial expression, tone and so forth. They can also identify contradiction between gestures and spoken words.

It is so exhausting to learn all this as a child. However, it is also important for them because it is the only survival technique they are aware of, which can help them avoid unnecessary pain. They grew up on the lookout for verbal, physical and emotional cues from narcissistic parents and caregivers.

This defense mechanism helps them get through a lot, and protects them from the unknown. However, it also breeds a sense of prediction, which can be very unsettling for someone who is genuine, but does not know how to align their words and gestures. For the child, it might be impossible to control how people react, but they can use this technique to choose the relationships they can cultivate or end.

- Afraid of intimacy

Intimacy is an emotional minefield for children raised by narcissists. When they try to open up, it is easier to share too much about their struggles in the hope that someone might feel their pain and genuinely ease their pain. The challenge here is that they often end up with toxic narcissists whose only desire is to prey on their weaknesses and exploit them for everything they have.

This is one of the reasons why such children are afraid of intimacy later on in life. Intimacy requires that you open up to your partner. You have to be vulnerable around one another. You must allow your partner to see you for who you are, with all your weaknesses, embrace you and love you endlessly.

Exposure to so much hurt while growing up destroys the concept of intimacy for these children. Instead of allowing someone the chance to hurt them, it is easier to cut them off, close all avenues leading to their emotions (Yates, 2010). They crave intimacy like everyone else, but it is so huge a risk. At times the prospect of opening up to intimacy brings back nasty memories, and it is easier to forget about intimacy altogether.

- Affinity for toxic relationships

Toxic relationships are normal for children raised by narcissists. They have a lot of experience in this, and it is easier to embrace these relationships because they almost always know what to expect. They embrace abuse as a normal thing, and that is why they find it easier to entertain people who belittle or envy them.

In early adulthood or later on in life when they take stock of their friendships and relationships, they realize they have so many toxic people in their lives that they are comfortable around. This happens because they share a bond. The struggle is all too familiar, it is the only thing they know.

- Emotional sabotage

Narcissistic parents create an unhealthy relationship with their children. Children grow up afraid. They know one thing leads to another, and are pessimistic about some situations. Respect and true love are foreign to them. If they come across someone who loves them unconditionally, it can be unsettling.

What does it even mean to be loved without expecting something back? How does someone even do that? This crisis sets the stage for emotional sabotage. Unconsciously, the child finds a way to sabotage that relationship because it is too good to be real. The defense mechanism for these kids is usually that anything that cannot come too close to them cannot harm them.

It is okay to protect yourself, but at times it comes at a price. Many opportunities are lost, opportunities for learning, growth, careers, and personal intimate relationships.

Relationships

A narcissist is a living example of a myth. They are no more than make-believers. They have a concept of themselves that they hope you can trust and believe. It is all lies. Narcissism has a damaging effect on relationships. Relationships require effort from both partners. As a victim, your relationship is anything but a joint effort. A narcissist partner will turn your life upside down and by the time they are done with you, you might not have the slightest idea who or what you are.

One of the difficult things in a relationship is telling whether you have a narcissistic partner, or if they are overconfident. A narcissist will abuse you emotionally, leave you feeling worthless (Lee, 2018). The following are some of the signs of emotional abuse that you need to be aware of in a relationship with a narcissist:

- Rationalizing the abuse

Abuse in a relationship hurts on so many levels. Victims of narcissists usually end up normalizing the abuse to the point where they deny it happening in the first place. You minimize and rationalize the problem. This is a survival mechanism that helps the victim dissociate from the pain of abuse. You get to a point where you feel your abuser is not a bad person. They had to react the way they did because you probably did something terrible to provoke them.

This kind of abuse happens after the victim is conditioned to believe that they are helpless without the abuser. A narcissist will do all they can to ensure you rely on them for survival, and by this point, the relationship is one-sided, with the victim doing all they can to appease the abuser and meet their needs.

There are instances where the victim goes as far as shielding their narcissistic abuser from the law, instead of facing the consequences of their actions. To convince everyone else but themselves that they are doing okay, some victims are conditioned as far as posting happy photos and videos of their relationship on social media, while the real story is different.

- Fear of success

Narcissists do not just take away your happiness, they take away your life. At some point, you stop doing the things you used to love. Success becomes a myth for you, because it makes you happy, yet your partner hates it when you derive happiness from anything other than themselves. Talent, happiness, joy and everything else that interests you becomes a source of darkness, reprimand and reprisal.

As this continues, you become depressed, lose confidence, anxiety sets in and you learn to hide away from the spotlight, allowing your partner to shine instead. What your abuser is doing is not keeping you away from your wins because they feel you are not good enough; they do it because they are afraid your success will weaken their hold on you.

- Self-destruction and sabotage

A victim of narcissistic abuse will replay the words and actions in their mind all the time until it becomes second nature. You learn to associate certain actions in the relationship with violence and reprimand. You almost expect a negative reaction from your partner each time you do something. This amplification of negativity will grow into self-sabotage, and if your partner is a malignant narcissist, suicide might not be so far off.

Narcissists condition you to expect punishment for basically, anything. Their constant accusations, criticism and verbal abuse pushes you to a life of guilt and toxic shame, to a point where you give up on your goals, dreams, and feel worthless. You convince yourself that you are not worthy, and you don't deserve anything good.

- Unhealthy comparisons

Triangulation is one of the tactics narcissists use to manipulate their victims into submission. In a relationship, it gets worse because you end up comparing yourself to someone else all the time. When your partner keeps making you feel you are not good enough and goes as far as introducing a third party into your relationship, this is emotional terrorism. You have to fight for their approval and attention with someone else.

Comparisons are quite unhealthy. You see yourself in a different light. You wonder what they see in other people that they cannot see in you. You remember the days when your relationship was still new, and wonder how you let yourself go and became worthless. It is demeaning.

- Survival through dissociation

Detachment is a survival technique that many victims of narcissistic abuse embrace. Other than detaching from their partner emotionally, they end up detaching from the environment around them. You go through life like a zombie, unable to feel anything. Your life is a mess, and you are unable to connect your emotions to physical sensations. They each exist independent of one another.

When facing a situation of emotional distress, dissociation becomes your way of life. This is the brain's way of filtering out the emotional impact of distress and pain, protecting you from having to experience the full wave of terror (Torres, Vincelette, White, & Roberts, 2013)

- Fear of the unknown

People who have experienced trauma tend to shy away from anything that might relate to it, or symptoms of the traumatic event. It might be a person, a town, a building and so forth. As long as something reminds you of the traumatic experience, you are conditioned to avoid it altogether. The same applies to victims of narcissistic abuse.

Over time you learn to be careful about what you do and the things you say around your partner. You are happy when they are gone, but the moment they come back home, your life turns into one endless pit of darkness. Living a life where you are constantly walking on eggshells around your partner is so demoralizing.

You find yourself anxious all the time, worried that you might provoke your partner into a fit of rage. You worry about setting boundaries because your partner never seems to recognize them anyway. You want to avoid confronting your partner, and you do your best not to, but for some reason, they provoke you to get them worked up.

- Unhealthy compromises

In order to meet your narcissistic partner's needs, you have to compromise on your needs, emotional or otherwise. Everything about you comes second after your partner. Your physical safety also becomes less of a priority to your partner or yourself.

An individual who once lived a very happy and satisfying life ends up living purposely to satisfy the needs of their narcissistic partner. Many partners in such relationships give up their friendships, goals, hobbies and lives to satisfy their abusive partner. Sadly, the more you give up, the more you realize your partner will never truly be happy or satisfied with your sacrifices. It gets to a point where you have nothing left to give.

- Health problems

Many victims of narcissistic abuse develop health issues along the way. A victim who has maintained a healthy lifestyle will start gaining weight suddenly, while some will lose weight. It is also possible to develop serious health problems as a result of stress, because most of the time your body works too hard to balance your cortisol levels. Your immune system also suffers from the trauma.

Sleep becomes a challenge for such people in a relationship, because you don't feel safe sleeping even in your own house. You experience frequent nightmares, and are dazed most of the time when you recall the trauma you have been through.

- Self-isolation

In order to make themselves the center of your world, narcissists will try to isolate you from everyone else in your circles. Some victims are made to quit their jobs and stay at home. The problem with this kind of isolation is that it persists to a point where the victim embraces it. The abuse you experience is shameful to you, and because you don't want people to know about it, you self-isolate.

Society today is not a kind place. Many people blame victims instead of listening to them. When you try to speak up about abuse, people ask you why you were abused instead of listening to your cry for help. Misconceptions about unhealthy relationships, trauma from family members who see your abusive partner in a different light and law enforcement are some of the reasons that combine to make victims keep to themselves.

- Self-mutilation

Surviving a narcissistic relationship is difficult. Many victims struggle with anxiety and depression for years. A relationship that was once full of happiness, joy and the promise of an amazing future turns into hopelessness. Everything around your relationship becomes unbearable. Even if you could escape, you cannot. You have tried it before and your partner managed to get you back. The pain is too much and you feel it is impossible to survive another day. Victims embrace self-mutilation to deal with the pain, and in some cases, attempt suicide.

- Deep mistrust

When your partner, in whose actions you place a lot of trust, keeps letting you down, you start to believe trust is a myth. You cannot trust anyone. Each time you interact with someone, you believe there has to be something malicious behind their actions. Your partner has done a good job gaslighting you into rethinking your happiness. Other than developing deep mistrust for everyone else, you don't trust yourself either.

Narcissism among friends

We need friends to help us get through life. We make friends at different stages in life too. Some friends stay with us all our lives, and others fall off along the way. Like any other institution in your life, you need to realize when your friend is a narcissist who will take away everything you hold dear. Here are some of the things you need to watch out for:

- Energy drain

Think about how long you have been friends. Remember how amazing it used to be to hang out, do all kinds of silly things, or perhaps just enjoy each other's company? Suddenly, you dread hanging out with your friend because by the time you leave for your place, you are so drained.

It is common to have friends who are very vocal about their lives, the colorful stories about their experiences. However, all they need in your life is validation. This is to boost their ego, and make them feel good about themselves. In case you don't offer them validation or don't pay attention to them, you become a boring friend. Your friend is a narcissist!

- My way or the highway

Friendship, like any other relationship brings two or more people together. You share ideas, experiences and so much more. A narcissistic friend will always insist that their way is the best way. They will be quick to advise you, and failure to follow their advice often results in contempt. Do not be fooled into thinking they are out to help you. This is a manipulative tactic.

- Extreme generosity

There is nothing wrong with generosity. Friends can always volunteer to help one another from time to time. The difference between a genuine friend and a narcissist is that the narcissist will not stop talking about how they help you. They will tell this to anyone who cares to listen. You are nothing but a roadside puppy they picked up in dire need of help.

- Unhealthy trash-talking

Each level of friendship has its own rules of loyalty and trust. A narcissistic friend is only loyal to themselves. They expect a lot from you in terms of trust, but will stop at nothing to speak ill of your mutual friends. They share stories about your mutual friends that they have no reason to. It is also easier for such friends to frown upon the successes of your other friends, and even revel in their misfortunes.

Workplace narcissism

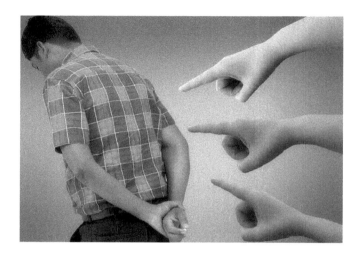

There is no place where narcissists tend to stand out more than the modern workplace. This is an environment where there is constant competition for recognition. People are always clamoring for the next promotion or contract. It is a cut-throat society out there, and one of the best places where you will experience the ugliest form of narcissism. How do you tell whether your colleague is a narcissist? Look for the following clues:

- Hoarding conversations

Narcissistic employees will always find a way to hijack a conversation, even if they have to interrupt. Their conceit comes from people discussing their lives, personal achievements, projects and so forth. If they come across people they know who are discussing something else, they will always find a way to make the conversations about them.

- Status and name dropping

You know that colleague who cannot wait for Monday to tell everyone about who they were hanging out with over the weekend? The senator they played golf with, the celebrity they went on a cruise with, the high end club they were partying at. These are signs of a narcissist. These are individuals who need to feel important, and as a result they keep presenting an exaggerated opinion of themselves. They have to be seen as the *it* person in the company.

- Salesman charm

Beware the typical salesman. Narcissists at work might be very persuasive and charming, but the one thing they never do is follow up on their promises (DuBrin, 2012). Many salesmen will promise you heaven on earth to get your signature on a contract. Everything else after you commit to the contract will be a nightmare. This is what some colleagues do.

When you meet them at first, they are impressionable. They make everyone believe in what they present. Those who are gullible will fall for the trick. However, they are notorious at missing deadlines, exceeding their budgets, and not meeting expectations. They are a burden in every group they belong to.

- Serial rule breakers

Narcissists at work believe they are too special to follow rules. It gets worse when they have a close connection or relation to someone in top management. They go about their business in the company as if they are not liable for any consequences. They want everyone else to see them as a special lot. It is not difficult for such a person to steal supplies from the office or doctor some reports to reflect something that is not true.

Part IV: Self-Healing

Chapter 7: Healing from Narcissistic Abuse

Overcoming narcissistic abuse is one of the most difficult things you might ever experience. It takes a lot of effort to find the momentum to jump from the pain that has engulfed your life to a better future. The most natural reaction to abuse is pain. Your life is shattered, your heart is broken, you lose everything. But all is not lost. There are solutions for you, effective solutions that will help you get your life back.

Meditation

Narcissistic abuse leaves victims in emotional trauma. The kind of trauma you experience in such a relationship has long-lasting effects on your life. One of the most effective ways of healing, managing and overcoming the negativity you experience from a narcissist is meditation.

Meditation is useful for virtually any condition that is either caused or exacerbated by stress. Meditation helps your body relax, in the process reducing your metabolism rate, improving your heart rate, and reducing your blood pressure (Huntington, 2015). It also helps your brain waves function properly, and helps you breathe better. As you learn how to relax through meditation, the tension in your muscles oozes out of your body from your muscles where tension resides.

The best thing about meditation is that you can perform it even when you have a very busy schedule. You only need a few minutes daily, and you will be on your way to recovery. During meditation, try and focus on your breathing. Listen to the air flowing in and out of your body. This action helps you focus by following the path the air takes in and out of your body. It is one of the easiest ways to calm down.

As the air moves in and out of your body, try and scan your body to identify the areas where tension is high. Observe your thoughts so you are aware of what you are trying to overcome through meditation. It is okay to feel the overwhelming sensations, but do not judge yourself. Recovery is not a sprint.

It might take you a few sessions, but your commitment will see you through.

Do not reject your emotions. Your emotions are a part of who you are. It is normal to react in a certain way to someone's actions or behavior towards you. Embrace the feelings and overcome the negativity. Meditation will help you make the neural pathways to and from your brain healthier and stronger by increasing density of grey matter. You learn to be mindful of your feelings and emotions again, and with time, you break the toxic connection you had with your narcissistic abuser.

Trauma and distress affects your brain by disrupting parts of the brain that regulate planning, memory, learning, focus, and emotional regulation. Over the years, meditation has proven a useful technique in overcoming these challenges by improving the function of the hippocampus, amygdala and prefrontal cortex.

As a victim of narcissistic abuse, once your abuser gets control over your life, you have nothing else but to follow their command. However, meditation gets you back in control of your life. You can reclaim your realities, heal and become empowered to overcome all challenges you experienced under their control.

Group therapy

Group therapy is one of the options you can consider when healing from narcissistic abuse. One of the first things you will learn in group therapy is that you cannot fix your narcissistic abuser. However, what you will learn is how to deal with narcissism.

Most of the time victims are encouraged to walk out of such abusive relationships, because there can only be hurt and trauma from them. Narcissists are ruthless in their pursuit of adulation, attention and gratification. They are aware that what they seek is impossible to achieve, so they delude themselves in the idea that they can make you achieve it for them.

Group therapy for narcissistic abuse is helpful because you get one thing you haven't had in a very long time, support. Each time you hear about the experiences of other group members, you realize you are not alone. The overwhelming feelings you have been going through become lighter, because you learn that there are people out there who can relate to what has been eating you inside.

While group therapy has its benefits, you will have to play your part to enjoy these benefits. Your willingness to heal is signified by the fact that you are taking the first step to seek help. Commit to the therapy sessions by taking a pledge of what you want out of it. Once you are in, participate. It might not be easy at first because you have to open up to strangers, but you will get the hang of it. It is okay to sit and listen to others tell their story at first. Once you feel comfortable, you can open up. Remember that it gets easier over time as you keep sharing. Never hold back. Therapy is a safe place. By sharing your experience, you are not just letting the group in on your pain, you might also be helping someone else in the group open up about theirs.

Cognitive behavioral therapy

Cognitive behavioral therapy (CBT) is a therapeutic process that combines cognitive therapy and behavioral therapy to help patients overcome traumatic events that have wielded control away from them. Cognitive therapy focuses on the influence your thoughts and beliefs have in your life, while behavioral therapy is about identifying and changing unhealthy behavioral patterns (Triscari et al, 2015)

CBT is effective because your therapist doesn't just sit down and listen, they also act as your coach. It is a healthy exchange where you learn useful strategies that can help you manage your life better. You learn to recognize your emotional responses, behavior and perceptions.

CBT is ideal for victims of narcissistic abuse because it helps them understand their emotional experiences, identify behavioral patterns, especially problematic tendencies, and learn how to stay in control over some of the most difficult situations in their lives.

Cognitive processing therapy

CPT is a subset of CBT. It is one of the most recommended methods of treating trauma patients. Victims of narcissistic abuse usually go through a lot of trauma, and they can develop PTSD. When you develop PTSD, you might have a different concept of the environment around you, your life and people you interact with. PTSD affects your perception of life in the following areas:

- Safety

After experiencing abuse, you are conditioned to feel unsafe about yourself and everyone else around you. PTSD can exacerbate these fears about safety. You are afraid you cannot take care of yourself, or anyone else.

- Trust

Narcissists break you down to the ground. They make sure you can no longer trust anyone, or yourself. In the aftermath, PTSD can cause you to not trust yourself to make the right call.

- Control

You don't just lose control over your life, you depend on your abuser to guide you through your life. Narcissism does this to you. Narcissists are happy when they have control over your life because it shows them they have your attention and can do anything they please with you. After leaving a narcissist, PTSD can reinforce a feeling of a loss of control, which makes getting back on your feet a very slow process.

- Esteem

One of the painful things about surviving a narcissist is the way they erode your confidence. Even some of the most confident people who have ever lived ended up unable to recognize who they are or what their lives are about anymore. You shy away from situations that require confidence and astute decision making, which you would have embraced willingly earlier on. Your perception of yourself is a broken, unworthy person.

- Intimacy

Among other manipulative tricks narcissists use, triangulation makes you feel so insecure about yourself and intimacy. You feel insecure because no one understands you, and at the same time, you cannot understand why they behave towards you the way they do. Following narcissistic abuse, PTSD may give you moments of flashbacks to the points when your intimacy was insecure. It can make it difficult to start new relationships.

All these thoughts end up in negative emotions clouding your life, like anger, guilt, anxiety, depression, and fear. Through CPT, you learn useful skills that help in challenging these emotions. The negative emotions create a false sense of being that embeds in your subconscious, making you feel like a lesser being. CPT helps by repairing your perception of yourself and the world around you. You learn how to challenge the abuse and gain a better, positive and healthy perspective of your life.

Yoga

For a trauma survivor, yoga can offer an avenue to healing. The restorative benefits of yoga have long been practiced in Eastern traditional societies for wellness. Yoga helps you establish a connection between the mind and your body. It helps you stay grounded. This is one of the things that you need when you survive a narcissistic relationship.

Yoga has been demonstrated in the past to be effective in treating different physical and mental conditions, trauma-related problems, and stress (Criswell, Wheeler, & Partlow Lauttamus, 2014). By combining breathing exercises, physical movement and relaxation, yoga helps you cultivate mindfulness and become more aware of your environment, internal and external.

Breaking up and walking out of a relationship with a narcissist is just the first step. Healing takes more steps. You need to find your bearings. You need to end the confusion that has engulfed your life to the point where you lack an identity.

During yoga, you will focus on breathing exercises. Breathing is one of the most effective and free ways of getting relief. Whether you are going through a difficult period, emotional upheaval or a moment of anxiety, all you have to do is breathe.

Each time you feel the urge to bring the narcissist back into your life, find a comfortable place where you can sit quietly and relax. Close your eyes and breathe. Focus on your breathing, counting your breaths to take your mind away from the problem. Gentle yoga classes can help with this.

Art therapy

Art therapy is founded in the idea that mental well-being and healing can be fostered through creativity. Art is not just a skill, it is also a technique that can be used to help in mental health. Art therapy has been used in psychotherapy for years. Art allows patients to express themselves without necessarily talking to someone about what they feel.

It is ideal for people who struggle to express themselves verbally. Art can help you learn how to communicate better with people, manage stress and even learn more about your personality. Through art therapy, experts believe that their patients can learn how to solve problems, resolve conflicts, ease stress, learn good behavior, develop or sharpen interpersonal skills, and increase their esteem and awareness (Lusebrink, n.d.)

Art therapists have a lot of tools at their disposal that can be used to help you overcome the trauma of a narcissistic relationship. From collages, to sculpture and painting, there is so much to work with. Art therapy is recommended for people who have survived emotional trauma, depression, anxiety, domestic abuse, physical violence and other psychological problems from an abusive relationship with a narcissist.

The difference between an art therapy session and an art class is that in therapy, the emphasis is on your experiences. Your imagination, feelings, and ideas matter. These are things that your narcissist partner might have conditioned you to give up. You will learn some amazing art skills and techniques, but before you do that, your therapist will encourage you to express yourself from deep within. Instead of focusing on what you can see physically, you learn to create things that you imagine or feel.

EMDR

Eye Movement Desensitization and Reprocessing (EMDR) is another technique that you can consider to heal from narcissistic abuse. It is a technique that helps to reprogram your brain away from trauma, so it can learn how to reprocess memories. Exposure to persistent trauma might see your brain form a pattern which perpetuates the negativity you have experienced for a long time (Mosquera & Knipe, 2015)

Traumatic memories cause victims a lot of psychological distress. EMDR is a unique method of treatment because you don't have to talk through your feelings and problems. The brain is instead stimulated to change the emotions you feel, months or even years after you walk away from a narcissist.

EMDR works because the eye movement enables the brain to open up, making it easier to access your memories in a manner that the brain can reprocess in a safe environment other than the environment in which your trauma was perpetuated. After accessing your memories, it is possible to replace them with more empowering feelings and thoughts, so that over time you dissociate from the pain and embrace more fulfilling responses to the triggers in your environment. Flashbacks, nightmares, and anxiety soon become distant memories as you embrace a new life and free yourself from their hold.

For victims of narcissistic abuse, your brain remembers the painful memories of verbal, sexual, psychological, emotional and even physical abuse. In an EMDR session, you are encouraged to focus on the details of any such traumatic events, while at the same time viewing something else for a short time.

What happens is that while you focus on both the negative memories and a new positive affirmation, your memory feels different. You will also learn self-soothing techniques to help you continue dissociating from the pain. EMDR helps to unchain the shackles in your life and allow your brain to think about experiences differently.

Self-hypnosis

Hypnotherapy has been used successfully to help victims of narcissistic abuse heal for so many years. There are specific conditions that must be met however, for this to work. You must ensure you are in the presence of specific stimuli that can encourage hypnosis. You will also learn how to narrow down your focus and awareness, and finally, allow yourself to freely experience your feelings without making a conscious choice to do so.

Narcissists are not capable of genuine connection, but instead they project their feelings and insecurities about loneliness and abandonment to their victim. How do you get into a trance state for hypnosis? Emotional abuse has a significant impact on your life. Hypnosis allows you to relax effortlessly. Effortless relaxation is one of the last things you might have experienced throughout your ordeal with a narcissist. The moment you are capable of allowing yourself to relax without struggling, you open doors to healing your mind and your body.

Self-hypnosis is a transformative process that restores your belief in yourself, encourages you to learn important emotional tools that can help you recover from abuse, and also help to protect yourself in the future. With each session, you become stronger, and calm. The waves of emotional upheaval you used to experience reduce and you become at peace with yourself and your environment.

Self-hypnosis also gives you a clearer picture of what your life is about. You let go of the negative vibes and embrace peace. You are set on a path to rediscovery. You find more value in yourself than you ever had throughout your narcissistic relationship. As you go on with these sessions, you learn how to take the necessary steps towards healing, and moving in the right direction in life. The most important thing behind self-hypnosis is that you start looking forward to a new life, and you actually believe in your ability to succeed while at it.

Aromatherapy

Even though it might feel like you are at the edge of a cliff and there is no way back for you, it is possible to recover from narcissistic abuse. Many people have done it before and you can do it too. Recovery from this kind of trauma is very sweet. Each time you make progress, you can look back at how far gone you were, and the changes you have made. It helps you appreciate your life, and realize how toxic it was earlier on.

Aromatherapy is one of the conscious efforts you take towards healing and recovering from narcissistic abuse. Think about aromatherapy in the same way you think about exercise. If you feel you are unfit, you exercise regularly. You can schedule three or four training sessions weekly to help you stay in shape.

The same applies to aromatherapy. Narcissists leave you so unfit emotionally. You need to get your emotions in shape so that you can live a happy and fulfilling life. To free yourself of emotional distress, you need to stimulate your amygdala. Smell is one of the best ways to stimulate the amygdala. There is a strong connection between your emotions and sense of smell, a connection that has been there since you were a child.

The sense of smell is closely associated with emotional connections, whether positive or negative. This explains why each time you smell your favorite food being prepared, it reminds you of an event during which you enjoyed it. Smell, therefore, helps to induce comfort, and nostalgia. If smells can take you way back, it can also help to remind you of the traumatic events that you suffered through narcissistic abuse.

Essential oils used in aromatherapy can help you access emotions buried so deep you never realize they are present (Kirksmith, 2004). They can also bring back memories so that you can embrace them and release those that are no longer useful. The difference between emotions and words is that while they both charge through your body, emotions are faster. It might take you a while to listen, speak and read something during therapy and allow your body enough time to process it. On the other hand, your body will respond to emotions faster. This is why most people are prone to making emotional reactions.

The following are some of the essential oils that can help you heal from emotional trauma, and restart a new chapter in your life:

- Basil
- Cedarwood
- Lavender
- Bergamot
- Lemon balm
- Hyssop
- Frankincense

During aromatherapy, you must remember that it is very possible you might not derive the same level of comfort from the essential oils as someone else did. If you don't like the scent of some oil, you might not get positive results from using it.

Chapter 8: Developing Emotional Intelligence After Narcissistic Abuse

Once you survive a narcissistic relationship, nothing is more important than healing. You have to learn how to regain your self-esteem and control. Recovery is not just about getting out of an abusive situation; it is primarily about creating a new emotional safety net for yourself. It is possible that it might take you a while to get over your trauma, but it is not the end of the world. Recovery is a gradual but efficient process. The following are some of the important things that you must keep in mind when working your way back into normalcy:

- Self-soothing and grounding techniques

A narcissist will confuse your concept of abandonment. If you have had issues with abandonment before, they will get worse during your relationship with them. The betrayal and subsequent abandonment makes you afraid. You feel you are abandoned because you are not good enough. There are negative emotions that can emanate from this, including panic, depression and sadness. Many victims make the mistake of turning back to their abuser because they have learned to believe they cannot survive without them.

Grounding yourself can help you overcome these problems. It is normal to feel like you lack something in the aftermath of this abuse. However, you do not have to react or respond to it by going back. Your amygdala might attempt to hijack your emotions from time to time, and the only way out is to remind yourself why you are not going back.

- Ask for help

You might not be capable of handling your recovery on your own, so seek professional support. In the wake of a narcissistic relationship, you often feel you cannot trust anyone to understand what you have been through. The rest of the world feels alienated from you. Instead of seeing people as a source of support, you feel they will judge you and you hold back.

At the end of an abusive relationship there are so many things that are left unresolved. You have a lot of unanswered questions, unfulfilled promises, unreciprocated love and affection. All these are things that you might not be able to deal with on your own. It is wise to get professional help so that you can understand yourself better, and manage your expectations better too.

The pain you feel at the end of this relationship is two-fold. You are in pain because the one person you invested everything on has turned out to be the worst investment of your life so far. You are also in pain because the relationship that you had so much faith in did not work out. You, therefore, need to heal from these two situations to completely heal and move on with life.

- Stay away from your abuser

Resist the urge to reach out to your abuser. Even if you miss them, stay away from them. Cut them off your contact list and forget about them. The confusion you experience will pass. One of the biggest mistakes that many victims make is that even after they are done with the relationship, they still leave room in their lives just in case their narcissistic partner can come back.

Forget about second chances. A lot of victims who go back to their abusers end up worse, and some end up dead. You don't have to reach out to them. Some narcissists will reach out to you after a long period of silence. They might reach out promising to change, telling you how things have been difficult in their lives since you left them. If you fall for this trick, you will never heal.

Whatever they do with their lives once you walk away is not your concern. They are adults and can make adult choices about their lives. You are an adult too, and your adult choice is to start afresh. The moment your abuser reaches out to you and you allow them a few minutes of your time, you are back to the very beginning. Never forget that narcissists always believe you need them more than they need you. They have a lot of tricks up their sleeve that will manipulate you back into their trap, if you allow them.

- Rebuilding your life

There are a lot of things that you can do to rebuild your life. Rebuilding your life is not just about reengaging people you had cut off, it is also about rebuilding your esteem and confidence. You have a lot of feelings bottled up inside. Don't keep them locked down, release them. Find different avenues where you can release your feelings.

Start writing, painting, gardening; or join a dancing class, an amateur sports team; and schedule social meetings with your close friends and have fun together. These are just a few things you can do to help you feel better again. Try and avoid risky or unhealthy behavior though, because these might end up in disaster.

- Accept your partner

You need to accept your partner for who they are. They are narcissists. They might be suffering from NPD. What acceptance does is to remind you that there is nothing you could have done to make them any different. They believe they are perfect the way they are. Since they cannot accept you as you are, it is best if you walk away and start afresh.

Accepting your partner's narcissism is another step towards forgiving yourself. You did all you could, but they could never change. There was never an intent to change in them. This will also help you overcome the feelings of self-doubt that you might have harbored for a long time.

- Forgiveness

Are you willing to forgive yourself for your role in the relationship? Forgiveness sets the tone for healing. Remember that forgiveness will only come after you have accepted your role in the relationship, and accepted responsibility for it. Everyone makes mistakes. It is normal to find yourself in a hardship situation out of your own doing. This is life, forgive yourself and move on. It is the things that you do and how you respond to these situations that will determine how your life turns out.

- Ease the pressure to recover

With your abuser out of the picture, there is a lot of pressure for you to recover and build a new life. Try to tone down the pressure. There is no time limit within which you must recover and start living a normal life. Your partner might have stolen your identity from you, but this does not mean you have to hurry to earn it back. Recovery is a gradual process. Everything around you takes time. You have to readjust to a lot of things in life, and if you rush it, you might be overwhelmed. It is okay to feel sorry for yourself, but don't let it turn into self-pity, or you might turn into a self-loathing individual. There is no race to recovery, it is a process.

Fundamentals of recovery from narcissistic abuse

There are four important tenets that will define your recovery process, and help you survive a narcissist. Everything else you do throughout your emotional journey revolves around the following:

1. Self-esteem

Self-esteem is simply you supporting yourself. You take back control from your partner, control over your emotions, your behavior, actions, your mind and your body. Everything that your partner took from you is back in your hands.

Esteem is not just about yourself, it is also about the way you interact with the environment around you. It is about how you respond to people, institutions and so forth. It is important to get back control over your esteem, because without it, you will continue on the destructive path of self-sabotage that your abusive partner had led you to.

You have to learn to speak positively to yourself. Don't hold back from pursuing things that appeal to you. If you had resorted to substance abuse to numb the pain of your abusive relationship, talk to someone about quitting.

Having lived through a life where you were afraid to try anything, it is time for you to motivate yourself to throw your hat in the ring. You might not be selected, but you challenged for something. Take back control over your life.

2. Self-love

No one will ever love you more than you love yourself. Loving yourself is about protecting the things that are dear to you. Nurture your feelings and emotions. You have to stop sacrificing your needs so someone else can be happy. Make yourself a priority. Let go of the tendency to abandon your needs for the sake of a superficial connection with someone else.

One of the ways you can go about rekindling your self-love is to realize the things that you can control in life and those that you cannot. Remind yourself why you feel it is necessary for you to change something in your life. For most ladies, one of the things they have to deal with is body shaming when they get out of a narcissistic relationship. You have to learn to accept and appreciate your body the way it is.

In case you are worried about things that you are unable to change, teach yourself to drown those emotions and sentiments instead. Find things that you are grateful for and enjoy doing them. If possible, do them with people who are close to you so that you remember just how amazing your life should be, and embrace it.

3. Self-trust

Fear and doubt are common in victims of narcissistic abuse. Your partner made sure the only person who made decisions in your life was them. They took away your ability to decide what you want or how you want things done. They became the ultimate source of power in your life. When you are unable to trust in yourself, you struggle to do things. You cannot make quick decisions because you are afraid you might choose the wrong thing. Your worry is that all the bad things you have experienced might happen to you if you decide for yourself. As a result, you second-guess yourself all the time.

Trust in your gut. Do something because you feel it is right. Don't hold back. To rebuild trust in yourself, you must take action. It is impossible to do this without stepping out and challenging yourself to try.

4. Self-worth

Why is it important that you rediscover your self-worth after walking away from a narcissistic partner? Self-worth is about realizing what your value is. When you understand your worth, it is difficult for someone to begrudge you what you deserve. Your value system sets you up high, and people who interact with you do so because they understand and appreciate how you treasure yourself. If you can't see your worth, no one else will. Even those who do will never take you seriously.

The challenge with lacking self-worth is that you usually end up compromising where you should not. Lack of self-worth also makes you feel ashamed and unworthy even without anyone provoking a reaction from you. You inherently believe you don't deserve the good things because you are not good enough.

Speak up for your rights. Don't shy away from the spotlight. Someone might use this to take advantage of you. Respect and take care of yourself. To rebuild your self-worth, you must embrace courage. You have to realize that even if things get difficult, you will make it.

Resetting boundaries after surviving a narcissist

Emotional abuse in a relationship usually comes with breached boundaries. You love a partner who doesn't recognize your need for or respect your space. People view boundaries in different ways. Their reaction to you having boundaries in the first place might not always be what you expect.

Some people react negatively, and others even turn cold towards you when you mention your boundaries. Should you back down? No, not at all. Boundaries are the essence of who you are. They are a representation of your thoughts, feelings and what sets them apart from everyone else. Boundaries are your ethical code, they determine wrong from right and give your life direction.

With boundaries, you can protect yourself from exploitation and manipulation. You also have limits to the things you can do for people. A narcissistic partner will usually break your boundaries. They don't respect you and this makes you feel unnecessarily vulnerable. At the end of that relationship, you should find a way to reestablish your boundaries.

The good thing about rebuilding your boundaries is that you also rebuild your esteem in the process, and as time goes by, you learn to love yourself again. You learn to trust and believe in yourself. How can you reset and rebuild your boundaries after such a traumatic experience?

- Rethink your values

Your core values are the foundation of your boundaries. Take time and re-examine them afresh. These are the principles and guidelines that control your life. They are the things you hold in high regard, like respect, honesty, affection, humility and loyalty. It is important to understand your values because they help you make the right decision.

A decision system should always be based on the things that align with your core beliefs. By understanding your values, you are in a better position to understand how to react or respond to different situations. You know what to do when facing a difficult situation. You know why it is important for you to walk away from someone because they don't fit in with your values.

These are decisions that do not just protect you, they also help you live a life you are proud of and you are at peace with your decisions. This way, you cannot second-guess yourself. If you have to make a big decision, you do so because you know it was the right thing to do. If it turns out wrong, you don't feel bad about it because you know it was still the right decision for you.

- Learn to say NO!

A narcissist will make you learn how to feel guilty each time you don't respond to their needs the way they want you to. Being a yes man or yes woman is exhausting. You never do anything for yourself. You never think for yourself. Your life revolves around what other people think or what they want you to do.

Learning to say no is not just about stopping someone from exploiting you, it is also about respecting yourself. It takes nothing from your humanity or personality to say no. Don't fall for the trick when someone tries to guilt you into believing saying no will appear aggressive or pushy. A subtle no is all you need, and stand by it.

To protect your boundaries, you must learn to be selfish. Your integrity is tested each time someone tries to have you go back on your no. Another problem you must overcome is the need to explain your reasons. A simple explanation is sufficient. However, if you over-explain yourself, this is a sign that you worry about what people think about you. It is a sign that you need to stop pleasing people all the time and be bold in your decisions.

At times, you don't necessarily need to explain your no. It might be a new experience for you, but give it time. It will grow on you. Some months or years down the line, you will realize it was one of the best decisions you ever made.

- Responsibility to yourself

Your responsibility in this life is to yourself. A life without boundaries opens you up to accept all manner of rubbish from your abuser and anyone else who can take advantage of you. You meet emotional wrecks who feel you can nurture them back to the person they are supposed to be. However, while you take care of them, they chip away at your personality and stability gradually.

You cannot be responsible for someone else's emotional wellbeing. If you allow them in, they will drain you. Why should you be exhausted from dealing with someone's trauma, and as they go away feeling happy and relaxed, your life falls apart because you can barely breathe?

While the emotional challenges you have experienced over the past might make you think you must take care of someone else's feelings, this is not true. Most narcissists simply project their baggage onto you and make you carry their weight alongside yours. You can understand them, but you cannot process the meaning and value of their emotions on their behalf. Step aside and let everyone deal with their own baggage.

- Respect your boundaries

There would be no point in setting boundaries if you were not going to follow through. Granted, this might be a new process for you, but it does not mean you will not hack it. For someone who has never had boundaries in their life, you must learn where to draw the line. You must be the first one to respect your boundaries before you expect someone else to do the same.

If this is your first time setting boundaries, start with simple things and learn to respect them. From there, build on to deeper stuff like your emotions. The discomfort you feel when rejecting someone because they don't respect your boundaries is normal. You are protecting something bigger than their feelings. Besides, they are responsible for their feelings. You are responsible for yours and your happiness.

To respect your boundaries and make them stick, you must be assertive in the approach you use. Don't bend the rules for anyone. This only makes you weak, and after a while, you will not respect your boundaries either. Everything that happens after you walk away from a narcissistic relationship is to help you become better. You are now in full control of your life, and you can steer it in whichever direction you please.

Conclusion

The environment you grow up in might determine so much about your life. For some individuals, it is because of their upbringing that they develop narcissistic personality disorder. When you are raised by parents who want to control everything in your life, it is possible their desire for control might have an effect on your life in the future. Some parents shed too much light on you, and it is difficult to fly under the radar.

Whichever reasons responsible for someone's narcissistic tendencies, understanding the person is the first step towards coexisting with them. Today a lot of people will advise you to stay away from a narcissist. Walk away from relationships with them and have yourself a happy life. However, what happens if the narcissist is your brother or sister? The rest of the world will avoid them because no one wants to deal with their inflated personalities. Do you walk away from them too?

Knowledge of narcissism can help you help someone who has narcissistic personality disorder. Granted, many narcissists believe that they are always right. No one knows better than they do. However, all this self-importance does for them is to conceal the real problem, the fact that they have deep insecurities that many people are unaware of.

Narcissists are just afraid that someone might find out the truth about them. Having created a persona of perfection, the fear that someone might know them too well and reveal their imperfections pushes them to survive. Survival tactics include manipulation by any means possible.

Even if you are not in a romantic relationship with a narcissist, close relations also suffer. A lover might walk away from your narcissistic brother or sister, but you cannot. You learn to live with them, because you have been there for one another since you were kids. There are always two sides of a coin.

In this book, we have addressed narcissism from three angles, the victim, the abuser and narcissism as a problem. Anyone who is close to a narcissist will find this book useful. In the example above, when the rest of the world avoids your sibling for who they are, it makes an already difficult life even more challenging for them. They feel like outcasts. What this does for them is that it heightens their need for self-preservation.

In such a state, their manipulation goes a notch higher, because they need to be loved. They have an urgent need to show everyone that they are not as bad as people think they are, and people are wrong to shy away from them. As a family member, understanding what they go through helps you learn how to manage your interactions with them. For validation, a narcissist will do and say anything to have you seeing them in a different light. Being alert to their manipulative traits can help you filter the drama, and at least maintain a semblance of a normal relationship with them. It might also make them realize that you are impervious to their manipulation, and probably have them recheck their approach.

On the part of a victim, there are tons of information in this book that can help you overcome your challenges. Psychological abuse is one of the most difficult things to get over. The uncertainty about your tomorrow or what happens next can cripple you. By the time your body embraces hypervigilance, you might have endured so much pain, you might not remember what a happy life is about.

As dark as your life might feel right now, the best chapter in the book of your life is yet to be written. You have what it takes to overcome the pain. The trauma will not last. You can take the first step towards freedom, by understanding why you need to walk away. You might feel you are always attracting narcissists, but it is not because you have a poor selection in partners, it is probably because you are naturally a kind, and sensitive person. It is out of the goodness of your heart that you meet someone. Unfortunately, some people are out to take advantage of you.

Self-preservation is one of the things that narcissists love. They will do everything to protect their interests and their interests always come first, above everyone else's. You too, can learn how to protect yourself. If you are an empath, learning to set boundaries and respect them is the first step. You cannot fix everyone. Some people are beyond help.

Don't give up. Never give up!

BOOK 2
EMOTIONAL INTELLIGENCE

Practical guide to master your emotions, improve your social skills and boost your EQ for business and relationships | overcome anxiety and unleash the empath in you

Introduction

Socially, there are individuals whom we admire. These are the people who always know what to say. Whether at work or at home, these individuals stand to be admired. This is because they always have a way of making people around them feel special and talking to them for a few minutes will give you a reason to be positive about your life.

Similarly, we have those people who are masters at dealing with emotions. You will never see them angry or rowdy. They always have a way of circumventing emotions which could make people see them as arrogant or proud. When faced with challenging situations, they have a way out. In spite of how strong they might seem, these individuals appreciate themselves for who they are. They know their weaknesses and their strengths.

Individuals with such attributes are emotionally intelligent. Besides mastering their emotions, they also see other people's emotions and can deal with them effectively. As we try to admire these individuals in our societies, deep inside, we hope for improvement. We anticipate that we will become better. Every day, people have high hopes that they could enhance their social lives. Without a doubt, most people love to be surrounded by friends and family. The people who we interact with remind us of our very natures. If you have a few friends, then you would obviously argue that you are an antisocial individual. On the contrary, another person will claim that they are friendly because of the huge social circle they have.

Owing to the varying personalities that people have, this affects the way they express their emotions. Also, the needs and expectations that we have will have a huge influence on how we express ourselves. Maneuvering past our personalities to express ourselves prudently, is never easy. It requires some form of cleverness, more so if you wish to succeed in life. Emotional intelligence comes in handy in such cases.

Briefly, emotional intelligence could be defined as one's ability to discern their emotions, understand them, and realize that they have a huge impact on those around them. Emotional intelligence also entails the perception that an individual has about other people. In this regard, when one comprehends how others are feeling, it gives them an opportunity to develop stronger relationships.

By taking you through what emotional intelligence means, this manual not only aims to help you master your emotions, but it also strives to revolutionize your social skills. This book will help you see past your interpersonal struggles and provide you with the right recommendations to enhance your social skills.

There is a lot that you will realize is possible to achieve. For instance, you might have been facing a huge challenge in gaining social confidence in front of others. Also, it could be that you have been suffering from the fear of rejection. Other people out there are just shy and socially anxious. At some point in life, we all have faced challenges as we try to socialize with people. For that reason, we need to understand how to master our emotions. It garners a deeper understanding of who we are and why we need people in our lives. Essentially, through emotional intelligence, our social skills are revolutionized. With time, we experience improvement in our conversations. Likewise, our relationships with other people are strengthened. So, we stand to benefit by being emotionally stronger. Let's take on this path together as we try to help you discover the power of mastering your emotions.

Chapter 1: What Is Emotional Intelligence and How it Affects Your Relationships

Emotional intelligence is a term which was created by John Mayer and Peter Salavoy. This concept eventually would be popularized by psychologist Daniel Goleman[1]. Emotional intelligence can be abbreviated as EI or EQ. The easiest way to understand EQ is that it refers to the ability of an individual to comprehend and manage their emotions and those of others. Those who have a high degree of EQ know their feelings. They know how their feelings could have an impact on those that surround them.

In our day to day experiences, emotional intelligence will imply being cognizant of our emotions and having the understanding that they could have a huge impact on our behaviors. People need to understand that their emotions can affect others either negatively or positively. More importantly, as part of improving their intelligence, they should effectively manage their emotions and those of

---

[1] "What Is Emotional Intelligence, Daniel Goleman - IHHP."
https://www.ihhp.com/meaning-of-emotional-intelligence. Accessed 4 Jun. 2019.

others.

There are a number of situations who one would want to manage their EQ. In your working environment, you should know how to give and receive feedback. When meeting tight deadlines, you will have to manage your emotions well. Your personal relationships also require one to handle their emotions appropriately. Say you are going through a change, this transformation will also demand that you keep your emotions in check. Therefore, emotional intelligence is applicable in all areas of our lives. Mastering your EQ will mean that you will increase your chances of succeeding in anything you do.

Elements of Emotional Intelligence

Emotional intelligence is composed of five major elements. These elements are briefly discussed.

Self-Awareness

EQ begins with self-awareness. Your intelligence begins with you. You ought to decipher your emotions before you can understand the emotions of other people. This is a fundamental aspect of EQ. Looking at the bigger picture, understanding your emotions also means that you are aware of the impact your emotions could have on other people.

Self-awareness can only be gained when you keep track of your feelings, moods, etc. Such monitoring requires that you evaluate how these emotions have an influence on how you react. Your awareness will also depend on how you recognize these sensations independently. Certainly, your mood will vary depending on how you are feeling. As such, being self-aware demands that you distinguish how these feelings differ.

An emotionally intelligent individual is able to gauge the relationships they enter into. Also, they can examine their behaviors from time to time. Notably, your self-awareness should give you the opportunity of knowing your personal strengths and weaknesses. With this personal insight, you can welcome new ideas to better enhance how you feel towards others and your overall wellbeing.

Conscious people are naturally funny. This is because they are confident in their abilities. Their confidence gives them a reason to believe that they can make people laugh. They are verbal as they know how to approach others with their ideas. So, for you to be regarded as emotionally intelligent, it begins with self-awareness.

Self-Regulation

Besides being self-aware about the emotions around you and how they can affect those you interact with, you also need to regulate these feelings. For you to be emotionally intelligent, you need to effectively regulate your emotions. No one can help you control your emotions better than yourself.

Self-regulation doesn't imply that you should hide your

emotions to yourself. Hiding what you truly feel is not the best way of managing your feelings. How do you self-regulate? Think about this as a way of modulating how or what you are feeling. This implies that you ought to be patient with how you express yourself. Know the right time to convey your emotions through your thoughts.

Simply put, self-regulation centers around the idea of expressing your feelings wisely and appropriately. You cannot lash out words just because you are mad over something. As an emotionally intelligent person, you should wait for the right time and platform to communicate your feelings. Eventually, you will have calmed the storm if you were dealing with conflict.

Social Skills

Part of being emotionally intelligent demands that you socialize with other people. Ideally, it wouldn't make any sense for you to comprehend your emotions and those of others and fail to use your knowledge practically. Therefore, EQ goes beyond comprehending your emotions and those of others. It should be evident. People should see it in you through your day to day communication.

Your remarkable social skills will be gauged through the benefits you will be bringing out. For instance, in the professional arena, as a leader, it will be seen through the meaningful connections you will create with other workers. Essential social skills that one should portray include verbal and non-verbal communication skills, active listening, persuasiveness and leadership skills.

Empathy

Another vital element of emotional intelligence is empathy. An individual should be able to show compassion about what others are feeling. You cannot be emotionally wise if you cannot understand what others are feeling. Empathy also goes beyond mere understanding. You need to take appropriate action depending on what you know. How do you respond to someone when you realize they are sad? For you to be empathetic, you have to respond.

Your response could be in the form of showing that you care for them. By showing concern, it proves that you are compassionate. Allowing empathy to grow in you gives you the opportunity of broadening your understanding regarding social relationships in different settings. In this case, you will be in a better position to know the factors which could highly likely lead to certain social issues. With this knowledge, you can accurately interpret how things could turn out. Equally, it would be somewhat easy for you to propose ideal solutions for people to adopt.

Motivation

At the bottom of the list lies intrinsic motivation. Your emotional intelligence will be gauged by how fueled you are to engage in particular acts. What does this mean? You should not be simply motivated by physical rewards. As such, you should be motivated from within. You need to be passionate about what you do. This means that you will be doing something with the mentality that there is a good feeling that comes with it.

In real life, you should set practical goals and strive to achieve them. Your motivation should not be set on the money you get or the fame that will come your way. Rather, it should be driven by your unending desire to improve and succeed in life. With such a perception, it wouldn't be surprising to associate emotionally intelligent people with success. These people are always out looking for a way to improve their lives. Moreover, they are usually committed to set goals.

Following what has been said about emotional intelligence, you know have a clear picture of what it means to be emotionally astute. The five key elements of EQ which will determine how smart you are should help you in knowing where you lie. First, ask yourself whether you are self-aware about the emotions surrounding you. You need to understand that your mood swings not only affect you but also those around you.

Beyond knowing how you feel, you should be able to manage your feelings. This entails knowing the best times to express oneself. Your social skills should also speak volumes about your level of EQ. More importantly, you should be empathetic and intrinsically motivated.

Chapter 2: Why Being in Tune with Your Emotions Can Significantly Improve Your Life in All Areas

In conjunction with what has been discussed in the first chapter, there are numerous reasons why you need to be in tune with your emotions. Reflect on the five elements of emotional intelligence as you read through this chapter. This will help you understand why it is essential to understand your emotions and those of others. With reference to self-awareness as an EQ element, consider whether you are aware of what you are feeling. Secondly, can you manage what you are feeling to guarantee that you are not overwhelmed? Do you feel motivated to get things done? Are you empathetic to other people's emotions?

Being in tune with your emotions requires that you have the right answers to the questions which have been pointed out. But, this chapter does not focus on whether you answered these questions correctly or not. Rather, it pays attention to the importance of portraying emotional intelligence. Essentially, the main question we are trying to put across is; why is it important to be emotionally intelligent?

Perhaps you have the perception that emotional intelligence will only benefit individuals who often communicate with others. Well, this is not the case. Generally, EQ will lead to a balanced life. This is because it helps in improving your life in all areas. Every aspect of your life will depend on how well you deal with your emotions.

Enhances Physical Health

Your physical health and wellbeing is closely tied to your emotional intelligence. Being physically healthy implies that you have to be ready to acknowledge the fact that you should be healthy. It begins with your self-awareness about your current condition. Equally, effectively dealing with stress is an integral part of being physically healthy. If you cannot cope with stress, this will have detrimental impacts on your health.

Improves Mental Health

Still, it goes without saying that stress will definitely affect your mental well-being. Aside from this, EQ will have a huge influence on your overall attitude towards life. Through emotional intelligence, you will have a unique way of dealing with depression, mood swings and anxiety. An emotionally intelligent person will have a different perspective towards life. This is because they will have every reason to be happy and enjoy themselves. Arguably, this has a positive impact on their mental health.

Leads to Better Relationships

Being in tune with your emotions helps you understand your feelings and manage them effectively. This understanding also stretches to knowing that your mood swings affects those around you. Keeping your emotions in check will guarantee that you experience blissful relationships with people. Ordinarily, people connect well with those who comprehend the feelings they are going through.

Consider the usual relationships we are often involved in. Usually, people are inclined to fall in love with those who care about them. Likewise, they become friends with individuals who are compassionate and welcoming. As such, emotional intelligence will transform one into a person capable of committing themselves to productive affairs.

Conflict Resolution

As previously discussed, EQ gifts one with the ability to recognize and take in personal emotions as well as other people's feelings. Therefore, it becomes easy to empathize with what other people are going through. Instead of entering into conflict, one would prefer to solve them amicably or simply prevent them from erupting from the get go. Equally, since one is in a better position to acknowledge the needs and preferences of those around them, they become good negotiators. In this case, it will not be difficult to offer third party individuals with what they need since they already are aware of the possible reasons for their predicament.

Increased Success

One of the main elements of emotional intelligence is that one ought to characterize a high level of intrinsic motivation. Taking this into consideration, EQ will highly likely lead to success. This is for the reasons that a smart individual will reduce their likelihood of procrastinating activities. Moreover, they have a high confidence in their abilities. This will have a positive impact on the projects they handle.

Similarly, your emotional intelligence will help you see past the physical rewards that you will get after achieving a set goal. Oftentimes, people are blinded by rewards such as money. We tend to focus on what we get in return after achieving a particular feat. Unfortunately, this drives us into obsessions. People end up developing the perception that money or fame will lead them to happiness. Truth be told, it never does. In fact, it leads to depression when folks later realize that they are not happy in spite of all the money and fame they have amassed.

Accordingly, emotional intelligence gives one a reason to see far beyond material benefits. Ultimately, there is a satisfying feeling that keeps one focused on their goal over the long haul.

Improved Leadership Skills

The potency to know what resonates with other people will undoubtedly lead to better relationships being created at work. Individuals with high EQs will therefore become better leaders. These are ideal leaders in an ordinary working environment simply because they understand the needs of other workers. Beyond this, they also know how their needs can be met without causing any inconveniences. In the end, this leads to a comfortable working environment where employees always feel motivated.

There is a greater value gained through emotional intelligence. Besides improving one's personal relationships, EQ can also help them deal with common physical and mental health issues. With the numerous benefits gained through emotional intelligence, there is a dire need to know how once can boost their EQ.

Chapter 3: How You Can Boost Your EQ

With the associated benefits of emotional intelligence, knowing how one can boost their EQ is essential. This is for the main reason that EQ impacts their lives in almost every direction. Your relationships, health, the professional world all depend on how well you recognize and manage your emotions. Therefore, you need to know how to boost your emotional intelligence. This section takes a look at the different ways in which a person can increase their EQ.

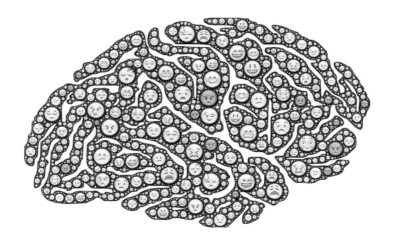

Reduce Negative Emotions

One of the main things you will need to work on as part of increasing your emotional intelligence is your negative emotions. It is important to make sure that you can manage any negative emotions which arise. The significance of doing this is that it guarantees that these emotions do not end up clouding your judgment. So, for you to effectively alter what you feel regarding a particular situation, you have to begin by changing your mentality about it.

There are instances where you might be irritated by the actions of your friend. In such situations, it is prudent to steer away from jumping into negative conclusions. It is vital for you to stop and look at the situation from different angles. For instance, say you tried reaching your friend by they didn't respond to your calls. There are two ways of responding to this situation. First, you might want to think that they were simply ignoring you. Alternatively, you could assume they were busy and that they will get back to you later.

The idea here is that you should try your best not to jump into negative conclusions. When you are emotionally intelligent, you are responsible for understanding others actions. means that you need to understand their actions. By taking a positive angle of looking at things, you prevent any misunderstandings from occurring.

Reducing negative emotions can also be attained by lowering the fear of rejection. Often, when things fail to work out as we expected, we are left devastated. To prevent yourself from disappointment, ensure you have multiple ways of looking at a situation. The significance of taking this perception is that regardless of what happens, you still have other options to anticipate. Consider a situation where you are applying for a job, When you put all your hopes in one dream job you applied, you will only invite negative feelings if things don't turn out as expected. Lower your fear of rejection by having other options. This means that if one fails to work out, you still have two other options to anticipate.

Stay Cool

People experience stress in their lives. The difference is how they deal with stress. The way you handle stressful situations will have a huge impact on whether you can be perceived as reactive or assertive. When pressure mounts on you, the best thing to do is to keep calm. This gives you room to think over a situation before taking any action. Making impulsive decisions will only spur trouble.

Adopt an Assertive Way of Communication

Adopting an assertive method of communication will assure that you gain respect from those around you. Being assertive means that you can confidently express your opinions without appearing rude or aggressive. It is vital for you to learn how to communicate your ideas without sounding pushy or too passive.

Active Listening

When interacting with other people, it is essential that you practice active listening instead of only waiting for your turn to talk. Listening is an integral part of any successful communication. It is important to understand what people are discussing before joining the conversation. The benefit gained here is that it prevents misunderstandings.

Equally, active listening requires that you should be attentive to non-verbal cues from those around you. Their body language can tell a lot about where the conversation is going. Actively listening will help you make ideal responses and that you will garner respect from those you are talking to.

Label Your Emotions

Another tip which could help you boost your EQ is the notion of labeling your emotions. You shouldn't be afraid to identify your feelings with specific terms. Most people will try to use different terms instead of simply labeling their feelings as they are. Instead of saying you had butterflies in your tummy; be clear and say that you were nervous. Labeling your emotions helps you to effectively understand how you are feeling. It raises awareness about your emotional state. Therefore, you are better placed to manage your feelings.

Take Critique Positively

Emotionally intelligent individuals understand that there is a good reason why they are being criticized. Instead of being offended, one should take criticisms positively. Taking a positive stand gives one an opportunity to comprehend how such criticisms could affect their relationships. Accordingly, any arising issues can be sorted out constructively.

Show Empathy

Most individuals will rush to argue that empathetic people are emotionally weak. Well, this is far from the truth. Showing empathy is a trait which shows that one is emotionally intelligent. In fact, it proves that one can understand what others are going through and help them with practical solutions.

Be Accountable for Your Emotions

A common habit that is evident in most people is the attempt to blame others for their emotions. Oftentimes, when you are feeling sad, you will want to argue that someone had the effect on you. What does this mean? Pointing fingers at others for how you are feeling simply means you are not in control. You are allowing other people to control your emotions. This is not an attribute of an emotionally intelligent person.

So, how do you refrain from blaming others? Well, before developing the perception that your only option is to blame others, pause and consider the fact that you are in control of your emotions. Give yourself a reason to understand that you can easily determine how you feel and how well you respond to other people. Knowing that you are in control gives you the power to determine the best way of responding to a particular situation. As you can see, it is all about reframing your thoughts.

Take Note of Other People's Feelings

Your emotional intelligence will also be evident through the way in which you react to other people's feelings. Before arguing with anyone, take a step back and try to understand how they are feeling. What is it that makes them react in such a negative way? Recognizing other people's feelings warrants that you interact with them on a more personal level. Also, it helps a lot to evaluate how other people's feelings can have a negative or positive impact on their behaviors.

Determine Whether Your Feelings are Friendly

Another effective way of boosting your EQ is by gauging whether your feelings are your friend or enemy depending on the situation you are faced with. Your situation will have a huge impact on how you will feel and possibly how you will react. After knowing exactly how you are feeling, weigh whether the feeling is your friend or enemy. For instance, if you are angry; your anger could be your enemy when talking to your boss.

In other situations, your sadness can be your friend as it could remind you of the importance of honoring something you lost. It could also be your enemy when it prevents you from seeing past your obstacles.

The significance of differentiating your feelings is that you will be in a better position to effectively regulate them. Taking time to meditate before making any moves will ensure you make the right decisions. Eventually, you will be walking on the right path towards boosting your emotional intelligence.

Track Your Progress

As you seek to boost your EQ, it is essential that you constantly reflect on how your performance was faring. When your day is over, take a few moments to reflect on how you interacted with your colleagues. Compare this with what you did yesterday or the previous days. If you see some improvement, then you are certainly headed in the right direction. In your relationships, consider whether you are gradually improving. You should notice a big change in how you interact with others. Monitoring your progress will confirm that you make necessary changes that will see you improve.

Advancing your emotional intelligence skills will certainly have a huge impact in all areas of your life. It will lead you to succeed in your professional field, relationships and your personal health. Thus, it is crucial that you adopt the strategies discussed herein to boost your EQ.

Chapter 4: Learn to Deal with Your Feelings

We all have emotions to deal with. Some of these emotions are easy to handle, whereas others are not. It could be said that feelings of joy and happiness are not difficult to handle. In fact, most people prefer to sail freely in these feelings and wish that things will never change. Unfortunately, the world is not like that. There are hard feelings that we have to attend to. These are feelings of anger, sadness, frustration, depression and the list goes on. Often, these feelings have negative impacts on our lives. At times, thee feelings lead people to taking their own lives.

Knowing how to deal with your emotions will make or break you. This section will discuss ideal strategies which can help you deal with negative feelings which may overwhelm you.

Suppressing Your Feelings

Most people will want to disagree with the idea of suppressing feelings, but it is one of the surest ways of dealing with your emotions. When you are going through a situation that could leave you embarrassed, the best way of handling such a situation is by suppressing your feelings. The same case applies to your feelings of fear. You need to learn how to contain them. It might not be simple to hold down such feelings, but try your best not to experience them. For instance, you could try getting yourself distracted with something.

Interrupting negative feelings helps you gain control of the situation. You are better placed to control the impact that these feelings could have. In the end, you will protect yourself from facing a huge loss which could have been caused if these feelings were allowed to take charge of you.

Unfortunately, the idea of suppressing feelings could fail. Yes, it might reduce the effects of a negative feeling, but it might fail to reduce how often you experience the emotions. Consider an example where a small boy is constantly bullied by a bigger boy in school. In this case, the boy might not show his fear, but he will still experience the bullying act.

Additionally, suppressing personal emotions is a huge challenge as compared to everyday events. For an individual to successfully contain personal emotions, they need to master self-control, something that doesn't come easily. Furthermore, there is a likelihood that the suppressed feelings will keep coming back and as a result, it could be difficult to keep up.

Timeouts

Dealing with your emotions can also be effectively achieved through taking timeouts. Usually, people in relationships take timeouts without actually understanding that they are doing it. When one partner rushes out of the room to some place quiet, this is taking a timeout. The importance of taking timeouts is that it breaks the negative course of a negative action. This means that it gives people an opportunity to cool down.

Timeouts will be effective more so when dealing with anger. If you find anger with someone or something, taking timeouts will help you think twice before worsening the situation. As such, don't focus on keeping up with the argument. Instead, take a break and interrupt the negative course of action which might have led to serious effects.

Stop and Think

The idea behind 'stop and think' is that one should implement a problem solving strategy to how they deal with their emotions. After determining how you are feeling, stop and take time to ponder on the impacts your feelings will have. Analytical thinking comes into play here as you are required to gauge the effects your emotions will have on you and those around you. When dealing with aggression, don't make hasty decisions. Instead, stop and mull over the repercussions. This will confirm that you find ideal ways of dealing with the situation.

Stopping and thinking is a strategy which will work simply because it also gives one the opportunity of calming down. As such, inappropriate feelings can effectively be dealt with. Giving your actions a second thought will guarantee that you make desirable moves.

See the Bigger Picture

Sometimes the best way of dealing with your emotions is by focusing on the bigger picture. You must have heard people arguing that everything happens for a reason. Well, it does. It is crucial that you focus on the good reasons why something is occurring. Yes, at times it might be difficult to see the best in everything, but it surely pays off. It gives you a reason to have a positive outlook towards what is happening in your life. Emotionally intelligent people will have the perception that failure happens to ensure that they perfect their paths to success. As such, you also need to develop such a mentality as it will drive you to succeed.

Understand Your Emotions

It goes without saying that the best way of dealing with a problem is by identifying what the problem is in the first place. In line with this, to deal with your feelings, you need to identify the feelings which are causing problems in your life. Ask yourself, what emotions are causing stress in your life? It could be your love life or your work life. Maybe you are feeling bad because you keep pushing everyone away because of your anger. The key to constructively deal with your feelings is by pointing out where the problem is coming from. This knowledge will allow you to make necessary changes in order to become a better version of yourself.

Pardon Your Emotional Triggers

Another strategy which will assist you in dealing with your feelings is by forgiving your emotional triggers. Emotional triggers are the factors which push us to the edge and make us angry, sad, or depressed. You know what we are talking about. Your emotional trigger could be your friend, neighbor or your ex-partner. Your friend could do something that you don't like and it could spur negative emotions. In such instances, you need to forgive. Forgive and disconnect yourself from the negative feelings. Give your friends an opportunity of being themselves whenever they are around you. By forgiving, you steer away from any negative feelings which could arise and worsen the situation. Therefore, the importance of forgiving your emotional triggers is that is brings a cloud of positivity in how you relate with other people.

Find Healthy Outlets

The importance of living a healthy life is a talk that never seems to end. If you have been keen enough, you must have heard that regular exercise will keep you mentally and physically healthy. Indeed, finding a healthy outlet to deal with your emotions will also help a lot. Exercise regularly as this will assure you of an emotional lift. Equally, taking time to meditate will help you find a way of focusing on the things you are grateful for. More importantly, have fun. Bringing joy to your life will attract positivity. You will find every reason to appreciate each day that comes. Do your best to find ideal healthy outlets which will help you focus on the good side of life.

Chapter 5: How to Control Negative Emotions

We are human beings, and therefore the emotional aspect of being human beings will always affect how we live. At any point in our lives, there are emotions that we have to deal with. We can choose to laugh or cry at whatever is happening in our lives. Unfortunately, negative emotions are the hardest to deal with. At times negative feelings overwhelm us to the point where we think of giving up. Learning how to control negative emotions will guarantee that we surround our lives with positivity. In spite of the things that we cannot control, we should be able to manage how we feel about them. Ultimately, this will have an impact on how we perceive our lives.

So, how do you control negative emotions from breaking you?

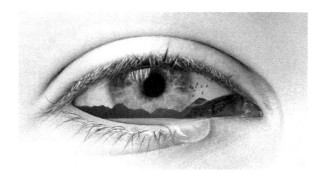

Eliminate Negative Thoughts

Managing negative emotions begins by eliminative negative thoughts. Negativity will always pull you down. You will always feel as though you woke up on the wrong side of your bed. Sadly, these feelings will also prevent you from seeing the good side of life. You will never see past obstacles that are stopping you from reaching your goals. Therefore, it is vital that you learn how to eliminate negative thoughts in your everyday life.

There are practical ways in which you could stop negative thoughts from affecting how you perceive things.

Talk to Your Negative Thoughts

The best way of dealing with your negative thoughts is not by avoiding them. Often, what you resist will persist. Therefore, it is essential that you become aware of these negative thoughts before anything else. How are you feeling? Are you tired, stressed, or frustrated? First, recognize your negative thoughts. To deal with them, embrace the idea of talking to these thoughts. This could be in the form of affirmations which remind you of the presence of the negative thoughts, but you are choosing not to believe in them. Ideally, affirming to yourself that you are in control will bestow you with the mind control you need to see past your challenges.

Associate with Positive People

Additionally, getting rid of negative feelings requires that you associate yourself with like-minded people. If you are trying to transform your life, find someone who is already in the position you wish to be in. Make friends and maintain your friendship. Identifying yourself with people who have a direction in life will also give you a sense of direction. You will begin to see the positive side of living. Therefore, you will refrain from thinking negatively as most of your friends focus on the bright side. With regards to emotional intelligence, find someone who is better than you. Learn from them on how to live an optimistic life. Ultimately, you will quash negative thoughts in your mind.

Lower Your Expectations

Indeed, it is good to live an optimistic life. Nevertheless, this doesn't mean that you should have high expectations. Expecting things to be perfect will simply prevent you from being happy. Your vision of success should be closely tied to reality. Knowing that you will succeed in the long run will give you a reason to be patient for the best results. In turn, you will never rob yourself of true happiness that you should be enjoying now.

Create a Positive Morning Routine

Psychologists will argue that controlling your thinking will help you control your life[2]. There is some truth to this. What you think about mostly, is what you will eventually become. So, start your day on a high note by encouraging yourself. This eliminates negative feelings and boosts your energy throughout the day.

Overcome Stress and Anxiety

Negative emotions will often lead to feeling stressed out and anxious. To manage negative feelings from arising through stress and anxiety, the following tips should help you.

Exercise Regularly

Regular exercise will help you deal with stress in many ways. The idea of pushing your body to the limits through exercise can really help boost your mental health. Research also shows that people who engage in physical

---

[2] "11 Ways To Stop Negative Thought Patterns And Move Forward - Forbes." 25 Apr. 2018, https://www.forbes.com/sites/forbescoachescouncil/2018/04/25/11-ways-to-stop-negative-thought-patterns-and-move-forward/. Accessed 5 Jun. 2019.

activities frequently will lower their chances of feeling anxious[3]. There are several reasons which could help in explaining this.

First, exercising lowers stress hormones in your body. Equally, regular exercise releases endorphins. These are chemicals responsible for enhancing your moods. Your sleep quality will also be improved through engaging in physical activities. The best part is that regular exercise will help you feel confident about yourself and your abilities. Inviting these good feelings to your life will definitely aid in eliminating negative vibe in your life.

Check Your Diet

Exercising routinely should be complemented by eating the right foods. The mere fact that you should overcome stress and anxiety implies that you ought to stay away from stress and anxiety triggers. Alcohol and caffeine, for example are known to increase the likelihood of feeling anxious[4]. Your caffeine intake should be avoided as this will make you feel nervous or increase your irritability. It

---

[3] "16 Simple Ways to Relieve Stress and Anxiety - Healthline." 28 Aug. 2018, https://www.healthline.com/nutrition/16-ways-relieve-stress-anxiety. Accessed 5 Jun. 2019.

[4] "5 Quick Tips to Reduce Stress and Stop Anxiety | Psychology Today." https://www.psychologytoday.com/intl/blog/finding-cloud9/201308/5-quick-tips-reduce-stress-and-stop-anxiety. Accessed 5 Jun. 2019.

is important to note that stopping your caffeine intake immediately will have negative withdrawal symptoms. Therefore, it is recommended that you should reduce your intake gradually.

It Shall Pass

Sometimes it is good to remind yourself that you are not the only individual going through stress in your life. In fact, some are going through harder situations. So, you need to brace yourself and keep your head up. Overcoming negative feelings that come with stress could be aided by having the mentality that the situation shall pass. The negative feeling that you are experiencing will pass. The important thing you need to bear in mind is that you are trying to make yourself stronger by believing that you can overcome the situation.

Overcome Social Anxiety and Shyness

Negative feelings can also be handled through the idea of overcoming social anxiety and shyness. The idea of being anxious when conversing with other people will invite negative feelings about yourself. You will never feel confident to approach people and express yourself. People will think that you are shy. From you end, you will suffer as you will always hide in your cocoon with no friends to help you out. Below are strategies which will help you conquer social anxiety and shyness in your life.

Admit the Fear

The first thing that you need to do is to admit that there is fear within you. Accepting the fact that you have that fear is an extremely important first step in overcoming your problems. You cannot deal with something or a condition without identifying it. The importance of acknowledging the problem you are facing helps in realizing that you are better than what you think. It gives you a reason of seeing past your fears or shyness.

Engage Actively

Fighting your shyness by engaging actively is an approach which could also work. If there is someone you like, approach them and be frank about it. Sure, you will be rejected a few times, but you will realize that there is nothing to fear. After all, there is no one who will be harmed from your rejection. You cannot expect everyone around you to like you. So, anticipate that there will be a few rejections you will have to deal with. Adopting this mentality gives you courage to overcome social anxiety.

There is nothing to be afraid of and that there is no harm in trying.

Get Out of Your Comfort Zone

Being shy will drive you to avoid people at all cost. Reserved people will prefer to be left alone in their own worlds. However, you need to challenge yourself. Engage in activities regardless of whether they make you anxious. Participate in social games as this is what will gradually boost your confidence levels. Don't allow your fear to get the best of you. Challenge yourself by facing your fears head on. It might be a daunting task from the word go, but eventually, you will rip the fruits.

Body Language

Your body language will also need transformation if you wish to overcome your anxiety. This will not come easily as you will have to practice regularly through the small conversations you enter into. When talking to people, try to make eye contact. Speak loudly for people to hear you clearly. If possible give hugs and shake hands. Working on your body language will boost your confidence in great ways.

From the information discussed in this section, dealing

with negative emotions is not as challenging as you might have assumed. It all boils down to what you think about. As part of making sure that you live a productive life, always ensure that you associate yourself with the right people. The influence you get from them will have a huge impact on your life. Similarly, you need to find a way out of stressful situations. Go to the gym and workout. Give your body and opportunity of releasing endorphins to help you feel good. Inviting positive vibes your way is an ideal way of banishing negative feelings.

Chapter 6: Tips and Strategies to Improve/Rescue Relationships in Both Your Work and Personal Life

Just to remind you, emotional intelligence will have an impact in all areas of your life. Learning how to deal with your emotions and those of others will help you live a purposeful life. You will always see the best out of every situation. When relating with other people, we always strive to present ourselves in a manner that guarantees we are accepted. Truly, whether at work or your personal life, we all yearn to feel welcomed and accepted. At times, the fear of rejection pushes us to engage in activities that we might not like. For instance, one could turn to drugs after a failed marriage. Also, it is common to see people getting depressed over their failed careers.

Undeniably, relationships are there to be mended. People are not born with friends. Folks should interact and find ideal ways of mingling. Having said this, it is imperative that you understand how to relate with people both at work and in your private life. The way you present yourself in front of other people will have an impact on the relationship you share with them. The following are recommended strategies which will help you in developing positive relations either at work or in your personal life.

Acknowledge and Celebrate Differences

Theodore Roosevelt once said - "the most important single ingredient in the formula of success is knowing how to get along with people[5]." To understand the process of best mingling and communicating with other people, you have to accept that we are all different. This is a pertinent reason as to why people find it challenging to blend with others. The innate differences that we have prevent us

---

[5] ""The most important single ingredient in the formula of success is ...." 22 Nov. 2015, https://medium.com/@steveagyeibeyondlifestyle/the-most-important-single-ingredient-in-the-formula-of-success-is-knowing-how-to-get-along-with-4f3babdc6c55. Accessed 5 Jun. 2019.

from successfully creating meaningful relationships. Usually, most people click when they gain the perception that they are understood. One will find it easy to interact with those that "get" them.

Nonetheless, it is essential that you steer away from such ideologies. Yes, you might be different but get it clear that the world would have been a boring place if we were the same. As such, accept differences and learn to celebrate them.

Listen Effectively

There is power in listening to what other people have to say. Psychologists argue that listening is a silent type of flattery. By actively listening, you give people the impression that they are valued. You are giving them time to express themselves without interfering. With regards to creating meaningful relationships, listening stands as a fundamental thing that you ought to do.

It is important to realize that you shouldn't just listen, but you should actively listen to what folks have to say. There is a difference here. Actively listening implies that you listen while also showing concern. Remember it is important that you express your understanding to what the other party is feeling or desiring. After knowing what they really want, you can move on to respond.

Give People Time

It is impossible to create meaningful connections with people without giving them your time. Giving people time is a special gift. Usually, we often claim that we don't have time. Therefore, by offering to spend time with friends, family and your colleagues, it means a lot. There is a lot that you will be sacrificing when you spend your precious time with individuals you care about. In the end, you find yourself developing strong bonds with those you interact with.

Unfortunately, the advent of technology has made it impossible to create worthwhile relationships. Today, most people will plan for a gathering where they get to spend most of the time on their phones. This means that their presence is not felt. Technological devices have robbed people of the value that they would have generated when others create time for them. Consequently, part of ensuring that you give people the time they need, you also need to make yourself present;

mentally and physically.

Improve Your Communication Skills

Communication is yet another key factor which will confirm that you create purposeful relations with people. A huge challenge experienced by most people in communication is that they make assumptions. Often, some folks tend to think that others have understood them. Making assumptions leads to misunderstandings and this negatively affects how people relate. At work, failing to communicate effectively could lead to backstabbing and blaming each other.

Good communication at work will have a positive impact on the overall morale of workers. In this case, when a leader conveys information clearly, junior workers will find it easy to follow instructions. Synergy will also be felt if at all people are working in groups.

Poor communication will also affect love affairs. Without understanding what your partner needs, there is a likelihood that things will fall apart. Successful relationships dwell on communication. Partners who always listen to each other will find ways of solving their issues amicably.

In reference to what has been said, an ideal way of rescuing or building relationships is through advancing your communication skills. How do you do this? Work on your body language, think twice before you speak, and have a positive attitude towards life. Indeed, there are numerous ways to improve your communication skills. Ensure that you take your time to learn and improve.

Manage Mobile Technology

The importance of managing how you use your devices is worth repeating over and over again. Most relationships have suffered because people don't know how to use their devices. In social gatherings, it is not surprising to find people glued to their mobile phones. Undeniably, this is not the best way of interacting with people. Sure, the use of mobile technology has transformed the way we communicate. However, the bitter truth is that it is negatively affecting our relationships. Consequently, something must be done. Change begins with you; learn how to use your mobile handset wisely.

Feedback

Communication will not be complete without providing feedback to those you are relating with. To create beneficial relationships, it is vital that you provide others with constructive feedback. Don't just respond without stopping for a moment to think. You want to evaluate whether what you were about to say is pertinent. about to say is important. Other people will value positive feedback from your end. This is an essential ingredient to building a strong connection with those around you.

There is always something to gain in the relationships we enter into. Having a positive outlook to any engagement you enter into will have a lasting impact. The best part is that you will live a happier life surrounded by people you love.

Chapter 7: Communicate More Effectively

The idea of effective communication always sounds that it is something innate. Surprisingly, it is not. When we try to communicate with other people, there are instances where things just go wrong. We say something to mean a particular thing but other parties get it all wrong. Unfortunately, this is what leads to misunderstandings. In extreme cases, it could lead to conflicts. Miscommunication can have negative effects in many ways whether at home or at work. Below is a look at recommended tips which should help you communicate more effectively.

Active Listening

One crucial fact that people should understand is that effective communication is more than just talking to other people. In fact, it is centered around active listening. This means that one should not just focus on what other people are saying. Instead, they should also pay attention to the feelings they are trying to convey. A strong emphasis is placed on engaging with the speaker and not just hearing what they are saying.

The significance of active listening is that is warrants that you can understand the speaker from a personal level. Equally, through engaged listening, the speaker garners the feeling that they are understood. Accordingly, this creates an environment for a stronger connection to be nurtured.

Non-Verbal Cues

A lot can be said about you through your facial expressions, gestures, body language, posture etc. These are non-verbal cues which should help you improve your style of communication. Learning how to study these non-verbal cues can help a lot in improving your connection with other people. Making eye contact, for example, will give your audience the impression that you are confident. Developing ideal non-verbal skills will go a long way in ensuring that you create meaningful relationships at home and at work.

Manage Your Stress

Communicating effectively also depends on how well you manage your stress. If you are experiencing negative emotions, it will be quite difficult to converse in a calm state. Therefore, there is a high chance that you will also aggravate the other party. Communicating in a calm state gives one the opportunity of evaluating whether they should respond or not. Moreover, they also find a way of responding without making the other party angry. In the end, this helps to maintain a stronger connection with those around you.

Assert Yourself

You should also adopt an assertive personality as a way of improving your communication skills. By being assertive, it means that you express yourself confidently. The way in which you communicate should give your audience the impression that you are a cool, calm and collected individual. Your level of assertiveness will give people a reason to trust you and the information you are sharing.

Keep it Simple

Another crucial strategy to adopt when communicating is to keep your message simple. Ensure that your message doesn't confuse your listeners. Don't assume that your audience will get what you are trying to say. Find a way of segmenting it for easier understanding.

Chapter 8: Develop Social Awareness and Build Strong and Meaningful Relationships

Social awareness will open doors for better and healthy relationships in your life. Also, it will lead to an increased level of emotional intelligence. For you to live a happier life, you need to be socially aware of yourself. People have all sorts of expectations concerning how they should interact with people. To most folks, they yearn to improve their relations with their loved ones. Other people seek for ways of increasing their social circles. All these relate to social awareness.

Social awareness is obtained through the notion of understanding what others are feeling through their words. When conversing with your friends, it is imperative that you can comprehend their emotions through the way they talk. Social awareness also implies that you ought to be conscious of your surroundings and how it can influence you. Increasing your social awareness will have a positive impact in your life as it will help you develop meaningful relationships.

Develop Empathy

An ideal way of developing social awareness would be by being empathetic. Your compassion towards other people will help you understand them better. You will know why they are going through a difficult time in their lives. Why should you be empathetic? Well, it is vital for you to be empathetic as it would open doors for genuine relationships. You will not just communicate with other people for the sake of it. Rather, you will be obliged to do it due to your considerate nature.

Evaluate Social Cues

Getting along with people easily also requires that you effectively evaluate social cues with those that you choose to interact with. Here, you are expected to master how to study body language, tone of voice, facial expressions etc. People will use their bodies to communicate in various ways. It is up to you to learn how to deduce what they are trying to say. For instance, the tone of voice used to talk to you could mean a lot of things. If someone is trying to talk to you politely, you can easily differentiate this from another who is talking rudely. Equally, the physical distance you share with your listeners will say something about your relationship. Individuals sharing intimate relations will be closer to each other as compared to those who are just friends. Of course, it would be strange to maintain close distances with your colleagues of opposite sex. The point here is that you need to learn what these social cues mean. Interpreting them effectively will help you develop close relationships with people.

Connect with Your Community

Your empathetic skills ought to be taken to the next level by connecting with the community. Get to know what other groups of people are experiencing out there. How are they expressing themselves? Social awareness, as earlier mentioned, centers around knowing the world around you. Take your time to mingle with people from other cultures. Don't just associate with your friends and relatives. Learn something new from individuals you have never interacted with. You will experience a totally different world from what you have been accustomed to.

Chapter 9: Improve Your Social Skills

Your level of emotional intelligence will have a huge impact on your social skills. Developing your social skills will gradually help you create meaningful relationships with other people. That's not all, you will also garner a fulfilling feeling knowing very well that people love to be around you. As such, improving how you socialize not only helps those around you, but you also stand to benefit.

Improve on Verbal Communication

People will gain varying perceptions about you just from the way in which you express yourself verbally. For instance, folks will jump to the conclusion that you are shy simply because of your low voice tone. Conversely, others will quickly see the confidence in you from the high pitched tone you have. Therefore, for you to improve on your social skills, you have to work on your verbal communication.

Additionally, you should also know how to initiate conversations. You cannot ambush people with topics they are not interested in. Learn how to initiate talks in a smart way and you will attract more people in your social circle. There are certain topics you should never talk about if at all if the person you are talking to isn't already close to you. For example, a topic on religion or politics could easily anger your listener.

Tweak Your Non-Verbal Communication

Besides learning how to verbally express yourself, you should also know how your body language can communicate to other people. To guarantee that you initiate conversations in the right way, always strive to use the right non-verbal cues.

Improving your nonverbal communication skills will also depend on how well you learn from other people. Learning from other people can help you a lot in knowing whether there are certain areas you need to improve to communicate effectively.

If you have not been smiling when talking to new people you meet, you need to improve on this. A smile is a smart way of proving to other people that you are social. Smiling when talking to new people will help them relax and feel comfortable talking to you.

Connect with the Real World

Connecting with the real world will give you an easier way of improving your social skills. For instance, when you go out to the gym, it would be easier to make friends than talking to strangers in the streets. This happens because you already share something in common. The same case applies to joining groups that have shared interests. Participating in community events, for instance, will increase your likelihood of making new friends. As you can see, it is all about positioning yourself strategically.

Practice Makes Perfect

Developing your social skills will also depend on how

frequent you practice. If you are not good with people, you shouldn't lock yourself indoors. Practice makes perfect. Go out to social places and mingle with people who have similar interests. Do it more often that you can imagine and expect better results to come your way. Keep in mind that there are times when people will brush you off. In such cases, you should not allow negative emotions get the best of you. Rather, have it in mind that not everyone can like you. It natural not to be liked by all the people around you.

Chapter 10: Improve and Enhance Empathy: Connect Naturally With Others

Giving a boost to your empathic abilities is an ideal way of increasing your emotional intelligence in the long run. At the beginning of this manual, we learned that empathy is a key element in emotional intelligence. For that reason, you cannot have a high EQ if you are not empathic.

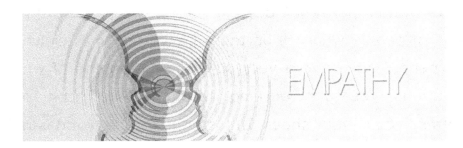

What is Empathy?

Empathy refers to an individual's ability to listen and comprehend what they are feeling. This is a virtue which is essential towards building strong relationships both at home and at work. People who lack this trait are often perceived as cold and distant. On the other hand, if you are an empathetic person, people will see you as loving and caring.

Common Traits of an Empathic Person

As you interact with people from all walks of life, there are certain traits which will tell you that you are dealing with a compassionate individual. Common personality attributes which will be evident in an empathic individual are briefly discussed.

Highly Sensitive

Guys with empathy will be highly sensitive. These are the kind of people who will be there for you no matter what happens. They have a very solid understanding of what emotions you are working through. They can put themselves in your shoes. Unfortunately, the world is not so friendly and therefore, such people often get easily hurt.

Highly Intuitive

Empathic people will want to face the world with the help of their intuition. Before taking any actions, they will want to follow their guts. The exciting thing about this is that they approach life confidently. At times, this helps them enter into blissful relationships simply because they believed in their intuitions.

They Give too Much

Being compassionate means that you can understand the emotions of other people. Therefore, a common trait of empathic individuals is that they love to give. Their act of giving is what drives them to help others out of their misery.

Need for Solitude

At times empathic people will be misunderstood due to their desire to be left alone. Their constant need for solitude is meant to help them connect with their inner selves. Eventually, this is what makes them self-aware of their emotions before understanding the feelings of others.

Improving Your Empathy

Considering the desirable traits of tenderhearted individuals, there are various ways in which you can learn to improve your empathy.

Get Feedback

Sometimes it is important for you to ask other people about your social relations. Don't just assume that because people are smiling at you, they are happy. Get honest feedback from your friends and romantic partners. They will help you identify areas where you need to improve.

Listen

Active listening can also play a big part in enhancing your empathy. Through listening, you get to understand people better and reason out with them.

Smile at People

Never overlook the power of smiling at people. A keen eye should tell you that smiling is contagious. Science tells us that smiling liberates chemicals in the brain which helps you maintain a good mood. As such, the act of smiling will not only help you increase health but it will also boost your empathy.

Scrutinize Your Biases

Equally, you should consider scrutinizing your biases. These are the factors which often prevent you from being compassionate with others. For instance, you might fail to connect people because you prejudice them based on their gender, age or race. To increase your empathic levels, try to examine your biases and find a way of ignoring them. Ultimately, you will appreciate the importance of seeing people for who they are.

Challenge Yourself

It is also essential that you get out of your comfort zone in order to understand people better. Don't allow conversations to end abruptly, challenge yourself by bringing in creative and interesting topics which will spur genuine talks. Ideally, you will connect with people far beyond knowing about where they live.

How Highly Sensitive People Manage Their Emotions

Most people will attest to the fact that it is not easy to deal with emotions. In fact, it is an overwhelming task. Empathic individuals are known to be highly emotional. However, it begs to wonder how they effectively manage their emotions.

If you are a highly emotional person, it is imperative to learn how to deal with your emotions. This will confirm that you are not blinded by your feelings. Truly, at times you need to wake up to reality. Before you can empathize with other people, you need to understand your boundaries.

Put Yourself First

Without doubt, putting your needs first might sound controversial because it is an uncommon trait of compassionate people. Nonetheless, for you to successfully take care of the needs of others, you need to begin by sorting your demands first. The idea here is that you should not be depleted. You should have the right energy to be able to see and help others out of their predicament.

Set Clear Boundaries

Sure, you are an empathic person. Nevertheless, this does not mean that you can help everyone around you. It is important for you to realize that you are also human; with flaws. As such, set clear boundaries to help you know when to stop. People should also understand that you have limits.

Let it Go

Indeed, compassionate people will want to walk in the shoes of other people and give them a shoulder to lean on in times of need. Similarly, when things are good, they will want to share moments of joy with them. In sad moments, it is imperative for empathic folks to learn how to let go. For instance, you might drain your energy when trying to mourn with a friend. In such instances, you need to embrace the idea of separation. There are some emotions that you need to separate yourself from. It might appear selfish, but in real sense you will also be helping yourself by managing your empathic nature.

Listen to Your Emotions

Another important step that empathetic people should remember to take is to listen to their emotions. You might be too focused on what others are feeling and you could end up forgetting about yourself. For you to understand other people, you should first begin by comprehending and managing your own emotions.

Practice Celebrating

An individual who often listens and understands other people, you know what it means to feel happy. Also, you are fully aware of what someone can feel when they are in pain. Unfortunately, negative feelings will stick around for long as compared to happy feelings. What you need to know is that carrying other people's negative feelings will not help you.

You should practice celebrating by reminding yourself of the good things you have achieved in your life. It doesn't have to be something big, honor any milestone you achieve as this will invite positive feelings you way.

Undeniably, having an empathic attribute will help you create blissful relationships with people since you can easily connect with them. However, you should also remember that you need to keep your life balanced. You need to pay attention to your feelings before committing yourself to others. First, manage your own before helping others.

Understanding the Potential of Being Empathic, Controlling Overwhelming Feelings

Besides people gaining the perception that you are too sensitive, there are numerous reasons why it is important to be empathic. Human beings can be unpredictable at times. When we watch the news and read the newspaper headlines, we often wonder how people can be so inhumane with their heinous acts. Building an empathic culture will, in the long run, help you grow your emotional intelligence. The mere fact that you can understand other people's feelings implies that you are emotionally smart.

Positive Vibe

There is a good feeling that comes with knowing that you have helped other people deal with challenging situations. Being empathic will therefore invite positive feelings to your life. You might not be rewarded physically, but a compassionate nature always pays off.

Develop an Identity

People will always have an identity to relate you with. If you are a cold person, they will simply know you for who you are. When in need of help, you can rest assured that most people will not want to help you. As a compassionate individual, you will develop a unique identity which tells a lot about how good you are. Again, this gives you a reason to be happy that you are making this world a better place to live.

Emotional and Physical Health

As people seek for ways of keeping themselves healthy and fit, they forget that empathy is a remedy. Well, this might sound strange since empathy is all about understanding people's feelings. Being empathetic means that you can learn more about how other people behave. Therefore, it gives you an opportunity of learning from others. By paying attention to people's feelings, you can adjust accordingly and live a healthier and happier life.

Additionally, connecting with other people is an important part of being a human being. Simply put, you have to create friends and learn how to live with them. Consequently, knowing how to effectively interact with others will keep you emotionally healthy as you can freely connect with those around you.

Lowering Stress

The virtue of being empathetic will also benefit you by helping you deal with stress. Bearing in mind that you can manage your emotions and those of others, it means you can handle stress better than other folks. You have been through tough situations since you have tried understanding others. Therefore, there is a high likelihood that you can challenge yourself and effectively handle stressful moments.

Conflict Resolution

Conflicts will always arise. This could happen in your personal life or at work. Sometimes it is difficult to deal with conflicts because our differences blind us from realizing why it is vital to compromise. An empathic person will listen and comprehend why others are angered. They will treasure the importance of finding solutions above anything else. Consequently, through their compassionate nature, they will prevent conflicts from escalating.

Supporting Socially Desirable Values

There is no single negative social value which could be linked to empathy. The idea of being empathic promotes socially desirable values. These are individuals who want the best for people around them. Their desire is to see people collaborate, understand each other, and most importantly, to heal themselves.

Accordingly, there is a great potential in being empathic. Some might perceive you as emotionally weak, but in the real sense, you are stronger. You are more in tune with your emotions and therefore, you can be recognized as an emotionally intelligent person.

The sheer fact that you can connect with others in a more profound way means that you create the perfect example of being a human being. Part of being compassionate means that you treasure connections over disconnection. Living and connecting with people is what defines us as human beings. Without the associations we have made to this point, we wouldn't have been where we are.

Final Thoughts

On a final note, mastering your own emotions is the surest way of advancing your social skills. Knowing that your emotions can have a huge influence on your relationships should drive you to learn how you can effectively deal with them. Individuals with high emotional intelligence know how to perfectly relate with others. These people are always careful not to let their emotions get the best of them.

Before pointing fingers at other people for your bad moods, you should understand that you are giving them control over how you feel. When you comprehend that you are the master of your own emotions, you will always be happy. Nothing will prevent you from living a happy life surrounded with people who express their love to you. Therefore, it is only through emotional intelligence that you can improve your life in all areas.

The elements of emotional intelligence tell a lot about what you need to do to boost your EQ. The first step you need to take is to be self-aware about your emotions. You cannot understand what others are feeling if you cannot comprehend your emotions. Through self-awareness, you will realize that your emotions will not only affect you but also other people. So, your EQ begins by first recognizing that it is vital for you to keep your feelings in check.

Comparably, you should work on self-managing your emotions. This demands that you should know the right manner of expressing yourself. In other words, you should know when to react and how to react depending on the situation you are faced with.

Another element of EQ is social skills. For you to consider yourself as emotionally witty, you ought to embody ideal social skills. People should see you as an example with regards to how you socialize with them. Your communication skills should define the type of person you are. More importantly, it should tell other individuals that you are an empathic person who is intrinsically motivated to succeed in life.

We all have emotions to deal with in our everyday lives. Whether at home or at work, there are emotions we need to manage. This means that our style of coping with these feelings will have an impact on our lives in many ways. For instance, when one is aware of their emotional abilities, they can tune themselves to share blissful relationships with others. Happy relationships can only be shared by people who understand each other. For you to live a happy life with other people, you need to begin by seeking joy within you. Consequently, this means that there is a dire need for you to boost your EQ.

Increasing your emotional intelligence not only helps you create meaningful relationships with other people, but it increases your chances of succeeding in life. How is this possible? Knowing how you feel and managing your emotions will develop a positive outlook about your life. You will always have a reason to live and see the next day. The strong bonds that you create with other people will motivate you to value experiences over material things. Your innate motivation will drive you to perceive life in ways that other people might not understand. To you, succeeding will not be an option but a necessity in your life.

Mastering your emotions will indeed bring many benefits to your life. Besides fostering meaningful relationships in your life, you will always gain from the desirable values you will be generating.

Bibliography

Bardi, C. A. (2015). Narcissism, Narcissism Everywhere. PsycCRITIQUES, 60(31).

Belikova, A., & Sue-Chan, C. (2015). What Inspires A Narcissist? The Role of Goal Orientation and Job Engagement. Academy of Management Proceedings, 2015(1).

Casale, S., Fioravanti, G., & Rugai, L. (2016). Grandiose and Vulnerable Narcissists: Who Is at Higher Risk for Social Networking Addiction? Cyberpsychology, Behavior and Social Networking, 19(8), 510–515.

Criswell, E., Wheeler, A., & Partlow Lauttamus, M. (2014). Yoga therapy research, individualized yoga therapy and call it yoga therapy. International Journal of Yoga Therapy, 24, 23–29.

DuBrin, A. (2012). Narcissism in the Workplace. Edward Elgar Publishing.

Freedy, J. R. (2016). My Wonderful Life: Reflections on Relationships, Empathic Connection, and Healing. Family Medicine, 48(5), 395–396.

Hart, W., Richardson, K., & Tortoriello, G. K. (2018). Grandiose and vulnerable narcissists disagree about whether others' vulnerable narcissism is relatable and tolerable. Personality and Individual Differences, 134.

He, N., & Zhu, Y. (2016). Self-love and other-love: Research on the relationships among narcissism, empathy and implicit altruism. Acta Psychologica Sinica, 48(2).

Houser, M. L., Horan, S. M., & Furler, L. A. (2008). Dating in the fast lane: How communication predicts speed-dating success. Journal of Social and Personal Relationships, 25(5).

Huntington, C. W. (2015). The Triumph of Narcissism: Theravāda Buddhist Meditation in the Marketplace. Journal of the American Academy of Religion,

83(3).

Huprich, S., Luchner, A., Roberts, C., & Pouliot, G. (2012). Understanding the association between depressive personality and hypersensitive (vulnerable) narcissism: Some preliminary findings: Depressive personality and hypersensitive narcissism. Personality and Mental Health, 6(1).

Huszcza, I., Berenson, K., & Downey, G. (2006). The role of rejection sensitivity in the emotional life of the covert narcissist: (511092014-144). PsycEXTRA Dataset. APA.

Jin-Won Yang, & Seok-Man Kwon. (2016). Emotional Characteristics of Narcissists with Grandiosity and Vulnerability. Korean Journal of Clinical Psychology, 35(1).

Keene, A. C., & Epps, J. (2016). Childhood physical abuse and aggression: Shame and narcissistic vulnerability. Child Abuse & Neglect, 51, 276–283.

Kirksmith, M. (2004). Clinical evaluation of aromatherapy. International Journal of Aromatherapy, 14(3).

Lee, J. Y. (2018). Emotional Exhaustion, Depersonalization, and Service Sabotage Among Customer Defective Behavior - Focusing on Aircraft Crews -. Journal of Human Resource Management Research, 25(2).

Lee, Y., & Park, J.-H. (2016). The Effects of Covert Narcissistic Personality Tendency on Somatic Symptoms : The Mediating Role of Perfectionism. Korean Journal of Youth Studies, 23(7).

Linden, P. (2010). Coping with Narcissism: Causes, Effects, and Solutions for the Artist Manager. Journal of the Music and Entertainment Industry Educators Association, 10(1).

Lusebrink, V. (n.d.). Art Therapy and the Brain: An Attempt to Understand the Underlying Processes of Art Expression in Therapy. Art Therapy Journal of the American Art Therapy Assoc.

Metzl, M. N. (2009). Book Review: How to Talk to a Narcissist: (597542009-018). PsycEXTRA Dataset. APA.

Miller, J. D., & Maples, J. (2012). Trait Personality Models of Narcissistic Personality Disorder, Grandiose Narcissism, and Vulnerable Narcissism. In The Handbook of Narcissism and Narcissistic Personality Disorder: Theoretical Approaches, Empirical Findings, and Treatments (pp. 71–88). John Wiley & Sons, Inc.

Mosquera, D., & Knipe, J. (2015). Understanding and Treating Narcissism With EMDR Therapy. Journal of EMDR Practice and Research, 9(1).

Newland, J. (2008). Respecting Personal Boundaries. The Nurse Practitioner, 33(8).

Ronningstam, E. (2012). Psychoanalytic Theories on Narcissism and Narcissistic Personality. In The Handbook of Narcissism and Narcissistic Personality Disorder: Theoretical Approaches, Empirical Findings, and Treatments (pp. 41–55). John Wiley & Sons, Inc.

Saltzman, C. (2009). Transforming narcissism: Reflections on empathy, humor and expectations. Psychodynamic Practice, 15(4), 426–432.

Schroeter, V., & Thomson, B. (2018). Chapter 7 – The Narcissist Character Structure. In V. Schroeter & B. Thomson, Bend into Shape: Techniques for Bioenergetic Therapists (pp. 113–134). Psychosozial-Verlag.

Stadler, J. (2017). The Empath and the Psychopath: Ethics, Imagination, and Intercorporeality in Bryan Fuller's Hannibal. Film-Philosophy, 21(3).

Stark, C. A. (2019). Gaslighting, Misogyny, and Psychological Oppression. The Monist, 102(2).

Torres, D. L., Vincelette, T. M., White, T., & Roberts, N. A. (2013). Traumatic Stress, Dissociation, and Relived Emotional Experiences: (594612013-001). PsycEXTRA Dataset. APA.

Trifu, S. (2013). The Malignant Narcissistic Dimension in the Antisocial Personality Disorder. Journal of Forensic Research, 04(03).

Triscari, M. T., Faraci, P., Catalisano, D., D'Angelo, V., & Urso, V. (2015). Effectiveness of cognitive behavioral therapy integrated with systematic desensitization, cognitive behavioral therapy combined with eye movement desensitization and reprocessing therapy, and cognitive behavioral therapy combined with virtual reality exposure therapy methods in the treatment of flight anxiety: a randomized trial. Neuropsychiatric Disease and Treatment, 11, 2591–2598.

Wright, K., & Furnham, A. (2015). How to spot a narcissist: Mental health literacy with respect to Narcissistic Personality Disorder. Personality and Mental Health, 9(2), 150–161.

Yates, A. (2010). Narcissistic Traits In Certain Abused Children. American Journal of Orthopsychiatry, 51(1).

5 Quick Tips to Reduce Stress and Stop Anxiety. (2013, August 25). Retrieved from https://www.psychologytoday.com/intl/blog/finding-cloud9/201308/5-quick-tips-reduce-stress-and-stop-anxiety

Agyei, S. (2015, November 22). 'The most important single ingredient in the formula of success is knowing how to get along with? Retrieved from https://medium.com/@steveagyeibeyondlifestyle/the-most-important-single-ingredient-in-the-formula-of-success-is-knowing-how-to-get-along-with-4f3babdc6c55

Forbes Coaches Council. (2018, April 25). 11 Ways To Stop Negative Thought Patterns And Move Forward. Retrieved from https://www.forbes.com/sites/forbescoachescouncil/2018/04/25/11-ways-to-stop-negative-thought-patterns-and-move-forward/

Kerri-Ann Jennings, MS, RD. (n.d.). 16 Simple Ways to Relieve Stress and Anxiety. Retrieved from https://www.healthline.com/nutrition/16-ways-relieve-stress-anxiety

CPSIA information can be obtained
at www.ICGtesting.com
Printed in the USA
LVHW021514220721
693417LV00025B/419